Tax Lien Certificates

A Little Known Government Program That Can Make You Financially Independent

By

Jim Yocom

ISBN: 1-4033-0835-7

This book is printed on acid free paper.

1stBooks - rev. 04/27/02

For my wife Barbara, who is truly
"The Wind Beneath My Wings"
and
For my brother David, who was
An inspiration for us all.

Introduction

I was looking at the *WALL STREET JOURNAL* dated January 20, 2002 a few minutes ago. The thought struck me that most Americans, who are making investments today, must be terribly depressed.

The story is pointing out that everyone knew last year was not too killing hot for investors, particularly in the stock market. What is depressing is that the article says that only now do they realize just how bad it was.

The news just gets worse. A little further down the page it points out that the transportation industry can look forward to an even greater decline this year: **183% below last year.** Basic materials are expected to decline 65% and technology stocks are expected to decline **another 70%.** Good grief!

Oh well, you can put your money in money market funds they are paying a whopping 1.51%. At least they are above zero.

For those of you who have been in the market and are still trying to get the red ink out of your veins, I apologize. I am not trying to pour salt in your wounds.

Years ago when I was suffering major brain damage in corporate America I told my support staff to never bring me a problem, unless they had thought about it enough to also bring their idea for a solution.

I have pointed out the problems with other investments. When you have finished this book, I know you will agree that I have brought you the best of all possible solutions.

The object of this book is to show you how to separate yourself from all the people the *Wall Street Journal* article was talking about. You don't have to be satisfied with the small returns and huge risks that are inherent in most investments.

You are going to learn how to outperform the greatest of the Wall Street hot shots. Not just this year. You can do it year in and year out. You can do it with just a little knowledge. You can start doing it with very little money. You can earn the same percentage on your small investment that the banks and credit unions earn investing millions.

How do you do this? More importantly, where do you do this? It is all in your hands right now. You can do this with an investment vehicle that almost no one knows anything about. It is called a **Tax Lien Certificate.**

I have tried to write this book just as I would talk to you in person. I have taken great liberties with the King's English, in some cases. My objective is to have this book judged for the information it delivers, not as a great work of literature.

If I can convince you, to convince yourself, just how simple it is to build a substantial net worth or even become rich, I have accomplished my goal. I want to give you all but the tiniest fraction of information you will need to accomplish your goals.

As you will quickly learn, there are a lot of variables associated with these investments. The variables are really just the procedural differences associated with the different entities offering and guaranteeing these investments.

I know of a lawyer who put all these minute pieces of differences in his work. It is in seven volumes. There is another that has a separate book for each state. Frankly, you just don't need this much information. The small differences that are not covered in this book are readily available with a phone call. Oh, and I have included the phone numbers.

Don't try to become an expert in every county in the United States.

Zig Zigler says, "You can suffer from a paralysis of analysis."

You gotta do this!

Jim Yocom

Chapter One

CAN I REALLY BECOME A MILLIONAIRE?

The way to make money is to buy a stock and when the price goes up sell it. If it doesn't go up, don't buy it.

—Will Rogers

Anyone can become wealthy! That's some claim. How many times have you heard someone tell you that if you just invest in their latest and greatest scheme, instant wealth would be yours? No wonder we are skeptical. We live in a country of instant coffee, instant tea and instant disbelief. Sometimes though, *just sometimes,* things really are just the way they are presented.

The book you have in your hands is one of these times. You are going to learn about the most highly publicized, best kept secret in America; Tax Lien Certificates.

Other than the book itself, I have nothing to sell. No one is going to try to sell you a Tax Lien Certificate. I will not gain one penny if you invest millions.

If you are a sophisticated investor you will certainly be skeptical when I tell you that you that you can make as much as 50% and more, per year on your investment, year in and year out. You will be even more skeptical when I tell you that this can be done with a higher degree of safety than anything you have probably seen.

1

But long before you finish this book you will know this is no great trick. There is no wizardry involved. You are going to learn, not only how to do this, I am also giving you a directory of where to do it. This is complete with name address and phone numbers of government entities who will sell and guarantee these rates to you with no one but you having any control over your investment, or getting a commission.

Here is an illustration of what you are going to learn to do. After you have studied this book try this.

WANT TO HAVE SOME FUN?
TRY THIS.

Go to a stock broker, real estate broker or anyone that sells investments. Or go to your banker for some advice.

Tell any of these people that you have some money to invest and you need some help.

Believe me they will break a leg to dust off a chair for you. They might even offer you coffee.

Now explain that your investment has to meet certain standards. If you can get a word in edgeways when they start assuring you that their particular investments are of the highest standards, you continue.

You explain that you want to control an investment portfolio of over $10,000,000. Now watch the drool drip off the chin.

"But," you say, "I only want to invest $130,000, but I absolutely insist that this gives me control of over $10,000,000 in assets."

As they sputter to explain that this just isn't possible you say, "Wait, I'm not finished. I also want to earn at least 24%. I want that rate of return guaranteed by the government to not go down. Also, I may want some of my investment capital to earn a guaranteed 50%."

Now it is no longer funny to them. They are ready to call security to get the guys in the white coats when you continue, "Just one other thing. In the event the investment doesn't quite work out the way we want, I expect to receive the $10,000,000 in assets to do with as I wish."

While they are waiting for the ambulance to carry you away they want to know where you ever got such a crazy idea. You say, "I do it all the time, don't you? I just invest in Tax Lien Certificates."

What? You think this is a bit outlandish? Not at all. Before you finish these pages you will learn that you indeed know how to do all the things outlined in this little story. And you will know where, and even have the phone numbers of the people who provide the investments and guarantee them.

Of course you could invest $1,300 and have the security of $1,000,000.

I decided to write this training manual in order to share just this kind of information with you. Information that I have spent a long time and a lot of money accumulating.

You are going to learn about an investment program that that allows you to be totally in charge. It is not subject to market fluctuations. Crooked investment advisers are not going to effect the market or the price. You are going to have the knowledge on your own, so you will have no reason to even listen to them.

When I first learned of the existence of Tax Lien Certificates, many years ago, I was astounded. I thought that I must have been caught in a time warp, or had lived in a cave for several years, and that was how I had missed out on this investment opportunity.

Far from living in a cave, I was a Financial Planner and had written a couple of investment training courses. I was traveling all over the country holding seminars to teach people how to make real estate investments with no money out of their pockets and how to really benefit from financial planning.

The light first came on for me one day when I was having lunch with two very heavy hitters in the investment sales business. Now, let me say right up front that both of these men are very ethical and honest.

During the course of our luncheon conversation these men began talking about the different investment programs they had been involved in over the years. Both men had been in the business for many years and had an extensive investment background.

At some point during our lunch, one of these gentlemen asked the other one how many of the investment programs he had been involved in had actually made his clients more money than they could have realized in a bank savings account. To recap a long conversation, both men to the conclusion that neither of them had ever been involved in a program that performed as projected.

Please understand they were not talking about anything dishonest. Every one of the programs they had sold were created by other ethical men who truly believed that their program promised significant returns to the investors. The programs were limited partnerships, real estate investment trusts, etc. They were not talking about individuals who were investing directly in the stock market, often with even worse results.

I was in a state of shock the rest of the day. If these men, who owned their own investment companies, had not been able to make any real money for their investors, what chance did the average investor have?

"WHERE ARE THE CUSTOMER'S YACHTS?"

Everyone has probably heard the story of the fellow who visited the home office of a large brokerage firm. Part of his tour included a tour of the fine yacht owned by the founder of the firm. After admiring this beautiful boat our fellow asked, "Where are the customer's yachts?"

According to my luncheon companions they just don't exist. I vowed right then and there that I would find an investment vehicle that was totally safe and would still offer large returns.

I studied everything I could find. In the course of this investigation I heard about Tax Lien Certificates. I wish I could tell you that a light came on immediately and I knew my search was over for the best investment vehicle.

Unfortunately, I didn't really look into Tax Lien Certificates and Tax Deeds until some time later, when someone asked me what I knew about them. That was when I began an earnest investigation of the possibilities.

I immediately went to the county library to find all the information available on Tax Lien Certificates. Guess what. Nothing. Not one book. Not one article. I also checked the university library with the same result. I called a few stock brokers and real estate agents, but none of them knew anything about Tax Lien Certificates either.

It didn't take long to realize why. Brokers can't sell Tax Lien Certificates and earn a commission so they have no reason to learn about them. Those that do know keep it quiet even though they may be investing in Tax Lien Certificates themselves.

You have heard the old adage about something being, "As plain as the nose on your face." Even though almost no one knows about tax lien investing, the auctions are advertised in newspapers every year. A recent ad in a Pima County, Arizona newspaper required 122 pages to list all the tax lien certificates available! And even though they guarantee 16% interest, thousands went unsold because people just didn't know what they were seeing.

This is not an isolated case. It happens every year all across the country. People just don't pay attention. (Neither did I before I started this search for information!)

Here we are almost at the end of 2001. Yesterday *The Wall Street Journal* showed that the average 30 month Certificate of Deposit is paying a whopping 2.88%. Six month CDs are paying 1.94%. Is this the way to get rich?

The more things change the more they stay the same.

During the time I was researching Tax Lien Certificates, years ago, the Dow Jones Average passed through 800 several times on its' way up and on its' way down. All in just a few short years. *(This will tell you how long ago my search began. Watch how many times the average passes through 10,000 now.)*

Gold and silver skyrocketed in price, then fell like a rock. Does anyone remember Nelson Bunker Hunt who tried to corner the silver market?

Investment grade diamonds had increased in value steadily for forty years. Then that market crashed and burned.

Real estate had gone boom and bust so many times that I lost count.

Oil was the latest craze. It was selling for almost $40 per barrel. There were over 4,000 drilling rigs in the U. S. running day and night and industry experts were predicting that oil would soon be $90 per barrel.

I abandoned my quest for tax lien knowledge for a time while I became involved in the oil business. I couldn't stand on the sidelines as a passive investor. I formed a company and bought a drilling rig. Within a few short months there were about 700 drilling rigs running, not 4,000 *(Mine wasn't one of the 700!)* and oil prices were in the $20 per barrel range.

Then came the real chaos. Banks failed. The savings and loan scandals rocked the nation with losses in the billions. Does anyone remember that George Bush has a brother named Neil who was head of Silverado Savings and Loan? That may be why we never hear about him.

Major airlines failed.

Chrysler required the help of the federal government to avoid bankruptcy.

Investors who had heeded the siren song of complicated tax schemes that promised tax deductions of $7 for every $1 invested were wiped out when the IRS said, "Not in this lifetime. Pay up!"

Life insurance companies had always been like "The Rock." Several major companies failed and others had to be rescued through mergers.

Through all these financial convulsions, knowledgeable investors were quietly building fortunes investing in Tax Lien Certificates with virtually no risk.

During this roller coaster ride little old blue hair ladies were playing cards with their friends while the Tax Lien Certificates they bought in the state of Arizona were earning them a guaranteed 16%. If they bought in Florida they were guaranteed 18% and other states were paying up to 24% year after year.

Texas sells an instrument similar to a tax lien that pays ***25% each six months.*** More than a 50% yield! And in Indiana it is possible to earn as much as 60%. None of these investors were drilling dry holes.

You gotta do this!

After the oil bust I actually saw a one cent sale on Lear Jets. Lear Jets were the real status symbols of the oil promoters. The promoters vanished along with the plummeting price of oil. So many planes were repossessed that a dealer at the Midland-Odessa, Texas airport was offering, "Buy the first Lear at the retail price and purchase the second one for a penny." None of our blue hair ladies who invested in Tax Lien Certificates had their Lears repossessed.

Do you think these times are over, *or ever will be?* As I write this we have just been through two extremely chaotic years in the stock market. The only thing that has changed from the real estate and oil and gas promoters is the title.

In recent history all a company needed was to have their company name end in **.com** and gullible people willingly threw money at them by the billions.

In the last few weeks we have witnessed the debacle of a high flier named Enron. What a mess! Due to political connections, greed and sheer stupidity this company's stock was selling at around $90 per share. Much of this was due to the outright lies of the company, and evidently the willing complicity of their auditors.

Employees were loading up their 401Ks with the company's stock. Why not? The CEO was telling them what a great deal this was just two weeks before they declared bankruptcy. They just knew they couldn't lose.

Then the bomb dropped. The shady dealing and number manipulation was exposed and the stock fell to less than $.50. Even the President's Mother-in-law sold her Enron stock, that she had bought for $8,000 for less than $90. This is a far cry from that heady $90 *per share* price.

As the stock fell, the executives unloaded and made millions.

How about Joe Lunchbox who was just an employee and had no part in the debacle? Did he sell his stock and hang on to at least some of his retirement money? I'm sure everyone knows the answer. The executives froze the employees retirement funds and they were not allowed to sell.

Do you think that the executives didn't want mass selling until they had gotten their millions? You decide. *No, wait, the courts will!*

One couple was interviewed on television who had over $600,000 in their 401K before the bankruptcy. Now how much? You guessed it. Nothing!

Well after the **.coms**, all the telecommunication companies and Enron, people have certainly learned their lesson. **_NOT!_** There were nine new stock offerings last week.

One of these companies saw their stock go up 50% the first day. Surely, that's better than Tax Lien Certificates, right? Read on.

This company has never made any money and according to the prospectus has no real plans to do so. So far this year the company as lost $31,000,000. *Don't despair, there are still almost three weeks left in the year. They may pull it out yet.* Last year they lost $33,000,000. The year before they only managed to lose $19,700,000. The year before that was a great year, they only lost $3,700,000. What a great bunch of guys.

It boggles the mind that investors were so anxious to throw their money into this pit that the price of the stock went up 50% just the first day. If they can manage to lose a billion no telling where this stock might go.

All this is happening while there are some 1,000 lawsuits pending against dozens of securities firms for manipulating stock prices.

Not only do you have to pick the right stock you have to pick the right broker. Over the last several months one 29 year old stockbroker swindled over $50,000,000 from his clients accounts and spent it on a Playboy model. He gave her houses, jewelry, **_an airplane,_** and something like 18 Rolex watches.

Does anyone with a double digit IQ really think they are going to sit in Podunk, USA and actually outsmart these guys? Dream on. And you think that the daily double at the track is a sucker bet.

Back to the old question, "Where are the customer's yacht's?" In this case, houses, jewelry and airplanes?

Go to Vegas. You get better odds and they give you free drinks while you hand them your money.

Or you can listen to all the financial planners. I have heard so many of them say the same thing recently that I think they all went to the same seminar. What is their educated advice? DIVERSIFY! Don't lose all your money on just one stock. Spread your money out over several stocks or best yet buy one of the mutual funds.

Now you have a really educated group of people who earn a fee to lose your money for you while you sit back in comfort.

THE GAME IS RIGGED AGAINST YOU

Don't think so? Here is an interesting choice. Let's say you have $10,000 and you are trying to choose between two stocks, and you can look into the future.

The first stock will go up 80% the first year and lose 50% the second year. Doesn't sound too bad. After all your **.com** had an 80% gain.

The other stock will go up 5% the first year and 5% the second year. This doesn't sound like much more than your bank savings account. Plus you had the risk of taking a loss.

Let's peek down the road two years. The first stock finished the first year up 80% so you have $18,000. Great!

The second year it loses 50%. Too bad, but you were already up 80% so who cares. You had better care because your $10,000 is now $9,000.

Stock number two is worth just $10,500 the first year and $11,025 the second year. Figures don't lie. Sometimes liars figure.

But, why should you be fiddling around with either one. If you had invested in Tax Lien Certificates in Iowa your $10,000 would have turned into $15,376 at the end of two years and would have doubled by the end of the third year. ***All the while it was guaranteed and secured.***

"Hold on." I can hear you say. "What do you mean guaranteed and secured?"

The interest rate is guaranteed by the government entity issuing the Tax Lien Certificates and they are secured by real estate.

Chapter 2

WHAT EXACTLY IS A TAX LIEN CERTIFICATE, ANYWAY?

There are no investment problems for investors in Tax Lien Certificates. The only problems are knowledge problems.
—Jim Yocom

Before we go on, lets find out just what this amazing vehicle is and how it can make all your financial dreams come true.

For probably as long as land ownership has been possible, governments have taxed the owners for the privilege of buying property with their own money. Most of the counties in the United States rely on property taxes for the great majority of their gross revenue.

Unfortunately, taxpayers do not always have money available to pay taxes at the time the government bills them. This puts a hardship on the county who is counting on these funds.

If this were the Federal Government; no problem. Just call down to the printing shop and print up however much they need.

States, counties, school districts, cities etc. can't do this. So they came up with an alternative.

As early as the 1800s local governments came up with a way to get their money right away. State Legislatures established a rate of interest to be assessed to the property owner who did not pay the taxes on time as a penalty, and an incentive to pay on time. The taxes and penalty assessments became a lien on the property.

These penalty interest rates vary from 6% to 50%, and you can even earn more. You will find out how a little later.

The local governments created a certificate evidencing this debt and the lien on the property. They were called **Tax Lien Certificates**. Because the taxing entity needed the money right away, they sold these certificates to investors. The Tax Lien Certificates conveyed to the investor the same penalties that were assessed and were due the county.

The local governments got their money right away from the investors. The investors were totally secured because they now had the same rights to the taxes and penalties that the government had before the sale.

In the event the taxpayer didn't pay the taxes the government had the right to foreclose and seize the property. The Tax Lien Certificates gave the investors these same rights. If, after a reasonable time, which is set by law in each state, the property owner didn't pay the taxes the investor could gain title to the property.

This has worked so well that more than half the states have legislation that allows counties and other taxing authorities to sell Tax Lien Certificates to investors.

HERE'S HOW IT WORKS

To understand Tax Lien Certificates you need to have a basic knowledge of real estate liens. For those of you who are already familiar with liens please indulge me. A property lien is defined as, "A hold or claim which one person or entity has upon the property of another as security for a debt."

Liens are recorded in the county where the property is located and are a matter of public record. Anyone can go to the County Courthouse and check on the liens recorded against any piece of property in the country.

Not all liens have equal power. They vary by seniority. The first lien filed has first rights to the property, the second filed has the rights to the property, subject to the rights of the first lien, etc.

For example, you gave a mortgage or trust deed, which are forms of liens, when you bought your house. The lender insisted that this lien had to be a first position lien to protect the loan.

In later years, if you borrow additional funds, using the equity in your house as security, that will require another lien. It will be junior to the original mortgage or trust deed. Should the senior mortgage holder find it necessary to foreclose on the property it will wipe out or eliminate all other liens and the senior lien holder will gain sole possession to the property, "Free and Clear" of all other liens. You will see how important this is.

A tax lien is superior to all other liens except IRS liens and most State liens. When a tax lien is filed against a property the owner cannot sell, trade or otherwise dispose of this property without this lien being paid.

15

If a property owner does not pay property taxes when due they become a lien that is superior to even the First Mortgage or First Trust Deed. So, should the county be forced to foreclose, the foreclosure will wipe out any claim that all lesser liens have on the property.

This is the reason your mortgage lender establishes an escrow account where you must deposit a part of your monthly payment. This ensures that funds are available when taxes become due and the lender actually pays the taxes out of this escrow account.

Enforcement of all the provisions of a Tax Lien Certificate are provided by the county and state where the property is located. The Tax Lien Certificate Owner does not have any contact with the property owner. When property owners pay their taxes they pay them directly to the county. The county collects all the penalties and interest and forwards all the money to you.

Actually, pretty simple.

YOU MISS OUT ON THE EXCITEMENT

Obviously, investing in Tax Lien Certificates is not nearly as exciting as some other investments. You will miss that breathless call to your broker, the race to check your computer or the financial pages to find out if you rolled a seven or snake eyes.

Your big anticipation comes from wondering if you are going to collect 50% or if you will wind up with real estate for pennies on the dollar. Pretty boring stuff isn't it?

One of my goals in writing this book is to explain how simple these investments really are. I want people who have never invested a dime in their lives to see that they can be more successful than the most astute Wall Street high roller. This is not meant to be a financial treatise. I just want to tell you a simple story just as I would if we were talking personally.

Buying Tax Lien Certificates is not a complicated procedure. You don't need to have a talent for picking the best certificate. Each certificate in a county pays the same as all the others. But, please don't think that you should go running to the next auction or mail a check to a County Treasurer without getting some education.

You are going to learn a very simple and safe way to actually become a "Cash Money" millionaire, if that is your desire.

This is going to require a little money, a reasonable amount of time, some effort on your part and a lot of knowledge. You'll find that knowledge in these pages.

EFFORT! SO THAT'S THE CATCH

Yes, you got me. If you are looking for an investment vehicle that gives you no say in how your money is invested, <u>this is not for you</u>.

Pick any ten mutual funds at random out of the paper and find out how well they have done over the last two years. If that appeals to you, <u>this is not for you</u>.

If you aren't willing to make a few phone calls from time to time to learn about the certificates that are available, <u>this *is not* for you</u>.

Are you going to have to study for weeks just to learn how to profit from these investments? No. Ninety nine percent of all the information you will need is in your hands right now.

Are you going to have to spend hours each day, week or month? Of course not. But you are going to have to put out some effort. No one is going to sell you a Tax Lien Certificate. You have to make the minimal effort to buy them yourself.

Should you invest in the stock market without acquiring some knowledge? Certainly not. If you don't know the difference between a closed end mutual fund and an open end mutual fund should you turn your hard earned money over to someone to buy them for you?

If you don't know the difference between an option and a warrant, or a put and a call should you be sending your money to someone to invest in a stock market you don't really understand?

If you are going to be a successful investor in anything you need to learn the basics. So why not spend your time learning about the investment that has the highest return with the least risk?

Makes sense to me, how about you?

WHAT IF YOU REALLY LIKE THE STOCK MARKET?

Maybe you are like a lot of people who are willing to take huge risks hoping for that tremendous pay off. Does this mean that tax liens are not for you? Quite the contrary. Why not build financial security through Tax Lien

Certificates, then gamble with the rest of your money, *if you must.*

Tax Lien Certificates can give you the comfort and assurance that even if you lose on your other investments you can still accumulate a fortune. Gamble all you like and you can still have a secure future.

Before you begin to learn how to be a successful Tax Lien Certificate investor, let's explore some ways this knowledge can be put to use.

For now the only thing you need to know in order to understand the concept is that you can make anywhere from 8% to 50% and more and be **totally secured.**

The percentages are different in different states. They are established by state law and are not subject to market fluctuations. *The interest rate doesn't go down!!* You know in advance what your interest rate is going to be so it is up to you to choose the state that pays the interest rate you want to receive.

Take a look at *illustration Number 1.* You will start to get a feel for what is possible. I want to show you some almost unbelievable accumulations and I want you to be comfortable with the knowledge that they are not dependent on luck or genius. I didn't make them up to impress you. Anyone can do this! The figures shown are just simple arithmetic.

You need to be aware of the power of compound interest. Albert Einstein knew a little about power; what with E=MC2, theory of relativity, time warps etc. With all that knowledge he once stated that the most powerful force in the universe is compound interest. Wow!

Everyone knows what compound interest is, but few people really understand the power of this wonder. For example; it would seem that if you earn 24% on an investment this should be three times the earnings you would receive on an investment that pays 8%. Look at the illustration and you will see that rather than three times the return on 8% in twenty years, 24% is actually more than 19 times as much.

Also 50% returns more than 26 times as much as 24% in the same twenty years. This is because each year you are earning interest on both principal *and interest.*

You can play around with some really wild, but totally accurate figures, just for fun. Try this. What if you invested $500 at the same 50% interest rate, but instead of a single $500 investment you invested $500 *per month* for the same 20 years?

At the end of 20 years you could start to withdraw your money at the rate of **$1,600,000 *per month for the next 20 years!*** And you thought only professional athletes and rock stars could get this rich.

Okay, we are getting a little carried away. You wouldn't want to make that much money would you?

But, is it possible? Why not? I'm sure not going to mislead you into thinking this would be easy. You would have to become a full time investor at this point. Bummer! What a way to make a living.

HERE BE DRAGONS

I do need to point out a couple of things. *Illustration 1* assumes that all your money is working all the time. There is one dragon lurking out there ready to destroy this plan. It is called the IRS, (It's called a lot of other things too!) and it is a factor that must be reckoned with. In order for you to realize these accumulations you will have to shield your earnings each year from taxes.

$500 invested one time and accumulated for 20 years
(Interest is figured at the end of each year.)

Year	8% Interest	24% Interest	50% Interest
1	$ 540	$ 620	$ 750
2	583	768	1,125
3	629	952	1,687
4	679	1,180	2,530
5	733	1,463	3,795
6	791	1,814	5,692
7	854	2,249	8,538
8	922	2,788	12,807
9	995	3,457	19,210
10	1,074	4,286	28,815
11	1,159	5,314	43,222
12	1,251	6,589	64,833
13	1,351	8,179	97,249
14	1,459	10,141	145,873
15	1,575	12,574	218,809
16	1,701	15,591	328,213
17	1,837	19,332	492,319
18	1,983	28,998	738,478
19	2,141	35,957	1,107,717
20	2,312	44,586	**1,661,575**

Illustration 1 shows some astonishing figures. It may not seem reasonable that just $500 invested continuously for twenty years at 50% interest could grow to more than **$1,500,00!** Try it with you calculator. *It's just arithmetic*!

You are in luck. Tax Lien Certificates qualify for tax sheltered plans such as IRA, SEPP, etc.

The simplest form, for your purposes, is a _self directed_ IRA. What is a self directed IRA? It is simply a plan that gives you total control of what you invest in and where your funds are invested. Not all investments qualify to be included in an IRA.

This must be a truly Self Directed Individual Retirement Account. A lot of mutual funds offer what they call a Self Directed IRA but these won't work. These plans are self directed only to the extent that you can choose between various funds offered by the same entity.

For example, you might be able to move back and forth between a Fidelity Money Market Fund and another Fidelity Fund that invests overseas. You cannot include an "outside" investment, such as a Tax Lien Certificate.

Contact a Trust Company or work with your CPA, if he is also a Financial Planner, to establish and maintain a true Self Directed IRA.

Since we are just having some fun with numbers, try this.

What would happen if you made the maximum contribution of $2,000 allowed in an IRA for the same twenty year period we have been discussing at 50%? It gets pretty exciting! At the end of the twentieth year you would have accumulated a total of *$13,297,027!*

Now it really gets mind boggling. *At 50% interest money will double in just a few days over 17 months.* So just 17 months later you would have *over $26,000,000!* The last time I checked this beats Social Security, hands down.

Just when you thought it was as crazy as it can get, try this. What if you and your spouse each had an IRA? You could invest $4,000 per year. Also in 2002 you can each put $3,000 in your IRA each year.

The 50% is available in Texas through what they call a Tax Deed Certificate. In a later chapter we are going to share some other strategies with you.

Can you buy this much property? Of course, there is a physical limit. There is certainly enough property available. The limitation is being able to get around to purchasing this many certificates. There are some large companies who do invest millions in Tax Lien Certificates. Who says you couldn't have such a company?

In order to have some quick fun with some of these figures learn "The Rule of 72" if you don't already know it.

This rule will quickly tell you how long it takes money to double at various interest rates. To find this period of time you divide the number 72 by the interest rate. For example: at 6% money doubles in twelve years. Just divide the number 72 by the interest rate, 6%, and you find that money doubles in 12 years at 6%.

Use the same procedure and you will find that at 10% your money will double in 7.2 years; 72 divided by 10 equals 7.2. At 50% it will double in 1.44 years, or just a few days over 17 months.

Conversely, if you want to know what interest rate you need in order to double your money in a certain time period, just work backward from the above example.

For example: you want to double your money in 3 years. What interest rate must you have? Just divide the number 72 by the number of years, 3, and it will give you the interest rate, 24%.

By the way, if you want a 24% interest rate, buy Tax Lien Certificates in Iowa and some parts of Maryland.

See how easy it is to plan your future now that you are getting the knowledge?

Sometimes it is fun to play around with some of the possibilities. The "Rule of 72" makes it easy. If you want to know why the number 72 makes this possible, study logarithms. Or, you can take somebody else's word. That's what I did.

DON'T GET HUNG UP ON TAXES

It is not the purpose of this book to do an in-depth tax study nor to develop a financial plan. But you certainly should have a financial plan that will show you how to make the most out of investing in Tax Lien Certificates. I just want you to be aware of what taxes will do to your accumulation plan and that there are alternatives available.

If you don't already have an excellent CPA, you need to get one. I'm not talking about someone who just prepares your taxes. You need someone who can do some serious tax planning and financial planning.

When selecting a financial planner choose one who works on a fee only basis and does not get a commission for selling investments. Just make sure they understand Tax Lien Certificates. It will be hard to find one so you may just have to loan this book to a planner who satisfies you in all other respects.

There are some tax sheltered plans that allow more than $30,000 per year in contributions. Play around with that. You need professional guidance, and you may need a bigger calculator. If you commit yourself to this you can make some serious money that warrants professional guidance.

Don't get so hung up on taxes that you think the only way to invest in Tax Lien Certificates is in a tax shelter.

Inside a tax shelter or outside, this is still the best investment I have seen.

My suggestion is to invest everything possible inside a tax sheltered program. Bear in mind, in most of these plans you can't take the money out until a certain age. So some investments will need to be made outside the plan. This is why you need a good financial planner and tax counselor that can minimize the taxes to be paid on investments outside the plan.

In most instances your Tax Lien Certificate investments are going to qualify for capital gains treatment so you will continue to have some tax relief. The point is, get a good CPA and follow his or her advice.

You gotta do this.

Jim Yocom

Chapter 3

SOUNDS GOOD.
TELL ME MORE.

Never invest in anything that eats, or needs repairing.
—Billy Rose

I have opened the curtain and you have peeked inside. Hopefully you are beginning to realize that with the proper knowledge, Tax Lien Certificates can, and probably should, play a major role in your financial future.

You have gotten a quick overview so now I want to give you the details of how Tax Lien Certificates work and how you can buy them.

You know that Tax Lien Certificates are issued when taxes are due on a property. These properties are assessed a penalty for being late. The penalty is in the form of an interest rate usually set by the state legislature.

Once the penalty has been assessed against the property this amount becomes a lien the same as the taxes. In order for the property owners to clear the title on their property they will have to pay the taxes *and the penalty, or interest rate.* Until these taxes are paid they can't sell, trade, or otherwise dispose of the property. In fact they can't even borrow against the property.

Occasionally someone will tell me that they don't want to invest in Tax Lien Certificates because they wouldn't want to take advantage of someone else's misfortune.

That is not the case at all. The taxes plus all penalties will have to be paid regardless of who owns the certificate; either you or the county. So the property owner is going to have to pay the same amount whether the county sells the Tax Lien Certificate to you or not. In reality, you are loaning that property owner the money to pay the taxes. The property owners are given plenty of time to pay their taxes before a Tax Lien Certificate investor acquires the property. Each state has established a ***Redemption Period.*** This is a period of time set by law, during which a property owner can pay the taxes, penalties, expenses and interest and keep his property.

This period varies by state as shown on this table.

REDEMPTION PERIODS SET BY STATES

ALABAMA - 3 years	ARIZONA - 3 years	COLORADO - 3 years
FLORIDA - 2 years	GEORGIA - 1 year but is not a tax lien state.(shown because of some unusual circumstances)	ILLINOIS - 6 months, 2years, 2.5 years
INDIANA - 1 year, 12 days for a county, purchasing agent or county having a consolidated city.	IOWA - 21 months	KENTUCKY - none
LOUISIANA - 3 years	MARYLAND - 2-6 months	MASSACHUSETTS 6 months
MISSISSIPPI - 2 years	MISSOURI - 2 years	NEBRASKA - 3 years
NEW HAMPSHIRE 2 years	NEW JERSEY - 2 years	NEW YORK - varies
NORTH DAKOTA 3 years	OKLAHOMA - 2 years	RHODE ISLAND - 1 year

SOUTH CAROLINA - 1 year	SOUTH DAKOTA 3 years for city property and 4 years for rural property	TEXAS - 2 years for homestead and agricultural but just 6 months for others. Texas is not a lien state but is shown because of some unusual circumstances
WEST VIRGINIA - 18 months	WYOMING - 4 years	

Don't start getting images of having to collect what is owed you, as a certificate owner, from a delinquent taxpayer.

There is usually no reason you would ever even meet the delinquent property owner. You will read about an exception to this in a later chapter. There is one circumstance where it can be to your advantage to contact the property owner.

The taxpayer deals directly with the county. When they pay their taxes, the county will notify you to return your certificate and the county will immediately send you a check for your original investment plus all the interest earned.

In most counties now they track the Tax Lien Certificates in their computer and you do not actually receive a certificate. You do receive a receipt showing that you are the owner of the Tax Lien Certificate.

When the property taxes are paid the county does not have to wait for you to return a certificate. This is much more convenient and it greatly reduces the time that your money is not working.

It is so simple. You buy directly from the county, the county collects your money and pays you. What could be better?

So far all we have talked about is Tax Lien Certificates. As you are aware by now, when you purchase a Tax Lien Certificate you are not acquiring real estate. You are just taking the county's place as the one to whom the taxes and penalties are owed.

In some instances you may actually acquire the real estate. More about that later. But, first you need to know about another way that some states collect delinquent taxes.

NOT ALL STATES ARE THE SAME

Twenty eight of the states sell Tax Lien Certificates which are liens on the property. The other states are called Deed States and actually sell the property itself for taxes.

These states present investment opportunities that can be as good, or in some cases, even better than Tax Lien Certificates. But, there is a completely different set of rules for these states. The most obvious difference is that there is no guaranteed interest rate so if you buy the property you are on your own.

HERE'S HOW IT STARTS

The county assesses taxes on property, called ad valorem taxes, which means they are based on the value of the property. They will vary, according to a formula, from one property to another.

The county starts with the *fair market value* (**FMV**). This is the actual value of the property if it were placed on the market for sale.

One of the ways the County Assessor arrives at this figure is by comparing the property to other similar properties that have sold in the area.

For example, a 1,500 square foot, three bedroom, two bath, double car garage house would be compared to similar houses in the neighborhood that have sold recently. These comparisons are called comparables, or *comps* in real estate jargon. There are other factors that enter into the appraisal process, but hopefully you get the picture.

The county uses another formula to arrive at what they refer to as a *county constant.* The FMV is multiplied by this county constant to arrive at an *assessed value.* This is the figure you are going to usually see on a county listing of Tax Lien Certificates offered for sale. Don't confuse this figure with the actual value of the real estate. In many cases the FMV is ten times more than the assessed value.

The county then takes the total assessed value of all the properties in the county, and the amount of revenue needed into consideration to arrive at a *mill* (**one tenth of a cent**) *levy.*

When this mill levy is multiplied by the assessed value of the property the county arrives at the dollar amount of taxes due.

This is a bit of an oversimplification. But, I want you to understand the principle, not make you an expert.

Here's an example. Assume for a moment that county has a county constant of .09 and the mill levy is .12. If a single family residence has a fair market value of $125,000 the county multiplies the value of the county constant of .09 to arrive at an assessed value of $11,250.

The point is, the fair market value in this case is more than ten times the assessed value. Around five times the assessed value may be more common.

Remember, don't confuse fair market value with assessed value. Now the county multiplies the assessed value times the mill levy of .12 to arrive at the taxes due on that property of $1,350.

Don't get too involved in all these formulas. I am only showing you how this works so you will know what you are looking at when you see a list of Tax Lien Certificates for sale. Since you are going to pay the taxes, I think you should know how they are figured.

You don't need to be an expert in this to be a successful tax lien investor.

WHAT HAPPENS NEXT?

Once the amount of taxes has been determined, a tax bill is sent to the property owner telling the owner the amount of taxes due and explaining the assessed value.

If the property owner believes that the bill is inaccurate or unfair the owner can go to the Tax Assessor's office and review the file on the property. In the file is a recent history of the property.

Things like, the size of the property, when it last changed hands, what kind of structure, if any, is on the property. etc. The property owner can find out how the county arrived at the amount of assessment.

If the property owner still disagrees with the bill in any way, there is a set procedure to be followed to appeal the assessment. Very often these appeals result in a lowering of the tax bill.

At any rate whenever the property owner is satisfied with the tax bill most of the taxes are paid promptly.

Most homeowners have a mortgage and the mortgage company collects money, as part of the monthly house payment, all year from the property owner and deposits it in an escrow account.

The mortgage company pays the taxes from this fund and most homeowners don't pay much attention to the entire process.

But, just because someone else is physically writing the check the property owner shouldn't neglect to check on the fairness and accuracy of their tax bill.

It is rare, but mortgage companies have been known to neglect paying the taxes when due. Ultimately, the responsibility of seeing to it that the taxes are paid is the responsibility of the homeowner. So check it out.

I know of an instance where a Tax Lien Certificate was purchased for $808.14 on a duplex with an appraisal of over $79,000. Despite all the notices being sent to the property owner the taxes were never paid. The investor obtained a Treasurer's Deed and owned the property. There was a handsome profit when the Tax Lien Certificate investor, now the owner, sold the property.

What makes the story so different is the original property owner. Guess who? It was you. Well, not you personally. It was the Federal Government. More specifically the Department of Housing and Urban Development, HUD.

Jim Yocom

Chapter 4

HOW DO I GET INTO THE ACT?

When you are young you think money is the most important thing in life. When you are old, you know it is.

—Oscar Wilde

When tax bills aren't paid promptly let's see what happens.

Different counties follow different procedures, even different counties within the same state.

First of all the state sets the rate of penalty that a taxpayer must pay for being delinquent. The procedures for collecting those taxes, and dealing with delinquent taxpayers, is usually left up to the individual counties.

Sometimes even the interest rate can vary from one county to another within the same state. For example; the State of Maryland allows the counties to set penalty interest rates and they can vary from 12% to 24%.

Obviously I can't detail the exact procedures of over 3,000 counties so I will explain what happens in general terms. You will need to check with the county where you want to buy Tax Lien Certificates for the procedure you will need to follow. You can get the address and phone number from your directory at the end of this book.

If the taxes are not paid on the due date you know the taxes become a lien against the property. Then a penalty is assessed against the property. The Tax Lien Certificates are offered for sale at a public auction, open to anyone, held in that county.

Usually, about one month prior to the auction, the county prepares a list of all the properties that have delinquent taxes and will offer a Tax Lien Certificate for sale.

The list of these properties is usually published in a newspaper of general circulation in that particular county. It is not always the same newspaper each year. Usually newspapers bid on the job of publishing that list. Sometimes it is several pages long.

You can, for a fee, get on the mailing list of the county that you are considering for purchasing Tax Lien Certificates. They will mail you a list of properties.

The lists used come in the form of a book or a reprint of the newspaper list. Now most counties have these on CD ROM.

I live in Adams County, Colorado. When this list came in book form it was usually over 100 pages and listed around 2,000 properties. It costs me $5 per year to have this list mailed to me about thirty days prior to the auction.

There is an instruction book that has a statement from the Adams County Treasurer, that explains the date, time, and location of the sale and the procedure that is to be followed at the auction. A copy of that statement and a discussion of the information contained in it will be shown a little later.

During the 30 day period from the time this list is published until the auction some of these taxes will have been paid. When you get to the auction you will receive a new, updated list.

THIS IS WHERE YOU COME IN

This is where the investor comes into the picture. At the auction the certificate is sold according to the procedures established in that county. This is a ***public auction*** with oral bidding. You will find individuals with very limited funds, credit unions and banks with many thousands of dollars in surplus funds to invest at the same auction. Both have equal access, though not equal funds. Anyone can invest.

WHAT DO I NEED TO GET READY FOR THE AUCTION?

First of all, you need to get on the mailing list from the county so you can receive the list and all the public information. This publication should give you all the rules of the sale.

You are wise and fortunate to be able to get some education prior to the sale. The rules of the sale that are found in some of these publications are just excerpts from the state statutes. They are often written in "legalese" by lawyers who seem to delight in making even the simplest things difficult to understand.

The county officials conducting the auction are not there to educate you on how the auction works. If you contact them prior to the auction you may or may not get much help.

While most county employees that I have met have been more than willing to bend over backward to answer my questions, they are sometimes prohibited from doing anything more than to give you a list of these rules of the sale.

You should look at the list and decide which parcels you want to bid on. After that, what you do next really varies by investor. (Aren't you surprised that this part isn't consistent either?) Some go to the courthouse and completely research these properties. They want to know the entire history of the property. But with thousands of properties for sale it just isn't possible to search them all. That's why you have to decide on the ones you may be interested in.

Part of that decision will be determined by the price of the lien. Part of it will be determined by the kind of property.

HOW DO I LOOK IT UP?

When you receive a list of the properties with liens you will need to reduce the list to the properties that meet your criteria.

If you are interested in buying liens on properties in residential areas you want to look at the legal description and find the properties that have the word **Additions** in the legal description if they are located in the city. If they are outside the city look for **Subdivisions.** These are subdivided properties and will include both residential and commercial properties.

ADAMS COUNTY 1995 TAX LIEN SALE
46

0171930218020   483   2157
GIBRALTAR EQUITIES LTD
LIABILITY COMPANY
8791 WOLFF   CT
   ASSESSED VALUE   23,490
   TOTAL DUE $2,196.13

0171930218021   493   2158
SHERIDAN REALTY PARTNERS
L P
8774 YATES   DR
   ASSESSED VALUE   529,250
   TOTAL DUE $62,452.11

0171930220021   493   2159
SHERIDAN REALTY CORP
C/O WILLIAM T ATKINS
8670 WOLFF   CT
   ASSESSED VALUE   466,320
   TOTAL DUE $55,030.36

0171930312030   555   2160
FJONE RONALD R AND
FJONE MARJORIE A
8003 RALEIGH   ST
   ASSESSED VALUE   9,310
   TOTAL DUE $858.31

0171930313047   555   2161
CRATER PEGGY J
8195 RALEIGH   PL
   ASSESSED VALUE   7,530
   TOTAL DUE $718.20

0171930314007   555   2162
BONATI EARL E AND
BONATI BARBARA L
8080 STUART   PL
   ASSESSED VALUE   9,710
   TOTAL DUE $921.25

0171930316002   555   2163
VEATCH FRANCES A
4220 W 80TH   PL
   ASSESSED VALUE   9,980
   TOTAL DUE $474.28

0171930402034   472   2164
STACKHOUSE ROBERT A AND
STACKHOUSE MARCIA K
VACANT
   ASSESSED VALUE   60
   TOTAL DUE $30.00

0171930406028   555   2165
MULLER HELEN L
8130 AUBURN   LN
   ASSESSED VALUE   8,640
   TOTAL DUE $820.90

0171930406030   555   2166
PONSFORD JOANNE D
VACANT
   ASSESSED VALUE   2,900
   TOTAL DUE $288.49

0171931106027   555   2169
MONTOYA GREGORY
7885 QUITMAN   ST
   ASSESSED VALUE   16,470
   TOTAL DUE $778.95

0171931110026   555   2170
KLAMN GERALDINE B
7921 MARIA   ST
   ASSESSED VALUE   10,570
   TOTAL DUE $998.11

0171931124030   555   2173
EMME DALE W AND
EMME R DARLENE
3899 W 76TH   AV
   ASSESSED VALUE   14,190
   TOTAL DUE $1,334.38

0171931203008   555   2174
CRATER GEORGE V
7928 STUART   PL
   ASSESSED VALUE   7,710
   TOTAL DUE $733.52

0171931210013   555   2177
FISHER RICHARD G JR
4318 W 78TH   AV
   ASSESSED VALUE   9,480
   TOTAL DUE $904.02

0171931213023   566   2178
LENZINI PAUL A AND
LENZINI LUCIA
7905 ZENOBIA   ST
   ASSESSED VALUE   22,020
   TOTAL DUE $2,183.21

If you go to *Illustration 2* you will see that Adams County, Colorado actually has the street addresses listed. This is not always the case. Many, if not most, counties only show the legal description.

The first thing you will need are maps to help you locate the properties. You can obtain plat maps from, sometimes several county offices; County Clerk, County Appraiser etc. You should probably start with the County Clerk. They can help you locate the maps.

You will also want a county grid map that shows the entire county if you are considering undeveloped land. These maps will show the Township and Range numbers. This map will help you locate each township in the county as well as location of undeveloped land.

The office that provides the map will help you understand it. It is their job, don't be afraid to ask for help.

Next locate every piece of property on the map that you have an interest in. If you have $3,000 to invest there is no point in locating properties that have $20,000 tax liens. You are now ready to drive by each property.

If you want to check on judgments or IRS liens you can ask the County Clerk, or County Recorder in some counties, to see the lien book and to show you where the IRS liens are filed. They are in alphabetical order by last names.

Personally, I am no longer interested in so much information. I mostly invest in Tax Lien Certificates with the goal of realizing a high return on my investment, not to acquire the property. The chances that I will actually acquire the property are really very slim anyway. There are better ways to acquire properties through tax sales.

If you are strictly interested in a high return you should buy liens on single family residences in decent parts of town. If they have a mortgage on the property you are almost certain that you are going to get paid off.

Investing for high returns, with a short pay off is still my priority. However I will also buy liens on vacant land.

40

There is a greater likelihood of actually winding up with the property. That is okay because I know a lot more about selling the property now.

One important item you need to check out is whether the property owners have either a Federal or State Income Tax Lien filed against them. These are the only liens that are superior to a property tax lien.

Just a quick note here. Often times in this book I tell you to check with the county officials on different matters.

You might wonder why I don't just go ahead and tell you how to do it yourself. There is a valid explanation. As you have already seen, so many policies and procedures vary from state to state and sometimes county to county within the same state. The explanation I give you may be good in one location and totally wrong in another. To give details in many areas would require explaining all the differences around the country and would require thousands of pages of really dull reading.

That having been said, the County Clerk will help you check out whether there are income tax liens filed.

Other than sometimes checking for these liens I don't do much else when I am buying Tax Lien Certificates on residential property. I am not advising you to invest this way. This is just my personal style.

ONE WARNING

If you are buying a certificate on vacant land and think you might wind up with the property, there is one thing you may want to check out.

There can be environmental problems. For example, if the property previously had a service station on it the gas tanks could have leaked and it can be horribly expensive to clean it up.

You can hire an environmental attorney to research the property for you. This too is expensive. It is easier to just stay away from property that can have this problem.

An excellent way to invest in Tax Lien Certificates with a better than average chance of acquiring the land is to buy certificates on property in resort or vacation subdivisions.

Often people buy these properties with the goal of someday having a vacation home or retirement home on the property. Circumstances change. Plans change. Sometimes the people, or their heirs, are just no longer interested in the property.

It is simple to get lots of information on these subdivisions buy just contacting the broker or sales office that is handling sales in these areas.

You will need to know how and when you will pay for the certificate. Does the county accept checks? Do you pay the same day you buy? Certainly, you want the date, time and location of the sale. These are questions that you want resolved before you do anything else.

You will also want to know how and when you receive your certificate. Many counties mail it to you within a few days after the sale. Others keep certificates electronically, rather in paper form. Some counties in Florida for instance, will keep the certificate on file electronically for you if you wish. You will have a receipt evidencing your ownership in the event you elect to let them keep it for you.

Tax auctions are held at different dates. Not all counties within the same state hold auctions on the same date. In most counties auctions are held once each year. In others it is more often. Are you getting the idea that there is no one set of rules that apply to all counties? If you are then you are getting the correct picture. Sometimes it seems that the only constant is inconsistency.

Actually this is great because it gives you the opportunity to find the investment that is just right for you.

I CAN'T GO TO THE AUCTION. AM I OUT OF THE ACTION?

Are you ready? I am going to give you another inconsistency. What if you can't, or just don't want to attend these auctions? Does this leave you out? Not at all. In fact you may even be better off. After the sale is over, if there are certificates left unsold, and there are in many counties, you can buy them over the counter by mail.

Recently, I visited the Treasurers Office in Pinal County, Arizona. They had a book of Tax Lien Certificates that had gone unsold. The book was 327 pages long. Each page had five or more properties listed. Any of these certificates could be bought without any bidding whatsoever and they all pay 16% without any bidding.

When we discuss the actual bidding procedures you will see that buying by mail may offer you the greatest return on your investment.

Don't let these inconsistencies bother you. The things we are talking about are procedural. The basic principles are the same.

You can contact the counties and most of them will mail you a pamphlet laying out all their rules and procedures. You will find lots of phone numbers in the directory in the back of the book.

OKAY, I BOUGHT A TAX LIEN CERTIFICATE. NOW WHAT?

Each state establishes a redemption period. The property owner must pay the taxes during this period or the Tax Lien Certificate owner has the right to foreclose and take possession of the property.

Sometime during this redemption period, most property owners come into the county and pay their taxes. As you know the county will collect all the money due, taxes, penalties, interest and expenses.

Some of your certificates may get paid off within only a few days. Others may not be paid off until the day of foreclosure. You will learn that the pay off date can really effect the yield on your investment. Sometimes negatively and sometimes positively.

You need to develop a plan to immediately reinvest the money from those that are paid off early. In some counties you can arrange the new purchase from the funds due you, in Iowa for instance. The object is to keep your money working all the time.

At whatever point the county collects the taxes they will let you know that the taxes have been paid and ask you to surrender the certificate. Then they send you a check for all the money due you.

In those counties that will keep the certificates on file, they just send you a check immediately, since they already have the certificate.

Because the redemption is set by state law it varies from one state to another. It can be as little as six months, or as long as five years.

This redemption period can really effect your chances of actually acquiring property.

WHAT IF THEY DON'T PAY?

One of the questions asked most often is, "Okay, the property owner didn't pay. I know I have to foreclose in order to get the property in my name. Isn't this a terribly complicated and expensive procedure?"

The short answer is, "No." First of all many counties will handle the foreclosure for you for a small fee, usually less than $500.

What if the county doesn't handle the procedure for you? Then you will need a local real estate lawyer to handle it for you. This is probably going to cost more, but bear in mind that you will own a piece of property for the amount of taxes owed and some legal fees.

Let's take a look at what you might be facing. Go back to our example of how a county assesses taxes on a piece of property. In our example the taxes on a residential property with a Fair Market Value (FMV) of $125,000 was $1,350. As you know, this will vary from one real estate market to another but it is a realistic representation in many markets.

What if you had bought a Tax Lien Certificate on that property and property owner didn't redeem the property during the redemption period? Now you are going to have to foreclose. You just hire a real estate lawyer to handle the procedure for you, if the county doesn't, and you don't even have to be there.

45

Be sure to hire a real estate lawyer. A guy who handles divorces may not be a great choice.

I am not going to forecast what a lawyer might charge you, but let's get totally outlandish and assume that it wound up costing you $5,000. It shouldn't cost anything even approaching this amount, I'm just making a point.

Even in this outlandish example, you will have $1,350 invested in the Tax Lien Certificate and after paying the lawyer, you will have a total of $6,350 invested.

When the foreclosure is complete you own a piece of real estate valued at $125,000 for a $6,350 investment. Don't you think a return of almost 20 times your investment is pretty good? Especially when your money was totally secured during the entire time.

If the legal fees were twice as much you would still be way ahead. Don't get hung up on something that appears to be a negative. There are no real "Gotchas" if you do your homework.

In some states you don't even have to go through a foreclosure process. In Colorado you apply for a Treasurer's Deed through the County Treasurer's office.

If you wind up with the property what do you do next? It is too obvious to say that it depends on the type of property that you get.

For simplification, let's say you wind up with the residence in the above example. (Don't hold your breath until that happens, but it has happened.) You have only two realistic options. Keep it as a rental property or sell it. But you already figured that out didn't you?

You want to think long and hard before you become a landlord. Does a phone call at 2:00 AM with, "Busted water heater" somewhere in the conversation give you cold chills? It sure isn't something that I want to deal with.

You will probably want to sell it. Especially if it is in a state or even city other than where you live. Most investors list the house with a broker at substantially less than the FMV in order to move it in a hurry. Oftentimes the broker will buy it, if it is priced correctly.

But bear in mind, this scenario will be a rare occurrence when investing in Tax Lien Certificates on properties similar to the above hypothetical case. You may just have to be satisfied with a return that would make most so called "Wall Street Gurus" mouths water. It's all in a days work for people like you who have this knowledge

ADAMS COUNTY TREASURER'S TAX LIEN SALE PROCEDURES

Date, Time, Location

The sale of the Adams County delinquent tax and special assessment liens will be held on October 3, 1996. The sale will commence at 9:30 a.m. and will be conducted at the following location:

Adams County Regional Park Complex, Annex, 9755 Henderson Road, Henderson, Colorado.

Deposits

All bids must be covered by cash, certified checks, bank cashier's checks, or personal check guaranteed by irrevocable letters of credit from the bank on which the check is drawn and deposited with the Treasurer prior to opening of the sale. **Bidders must make initial deposit in the Adams County Regional Park Complex, Annex, 9755 Henderson Road, Henderson, Colorado.** Deposits will be accepted prior to sale day at the Adams County Treasurer's Office, 450 S. 4th Ave., Brighton, Colorado.

Deposits must be made in the name which will appear on the certificate of sale and no transfer of deposits from one account to another will be permitted during the sale. When the deposit of a buyer equals the total consideration (taxes, penalties, costs, and premium [bonus]) stricken off to him, he shall no longer be recognized as a buyer unless additional deposits, in compliance with original deposit criteria, are made in advance of actual bidding. The excess of deposits will be returned as quickly as possible after the close of the sale.

SEATING

There will be no assignment or reservation of seats. Seating will be on the basis of choice upon arrival. Doors of the Annex Building will be open at 7:00 a.m. Deposits will be accepted beginning at 7:30 a.m.

Buyer Data

Each Buyer will be required to complete a form with name, address and telephone number. After the form has been completed and the buyer has provided proof of deposit, he will be assigned a bidder number and card.

Buyers are responsible to assure that the information is correct. Certificates, refund checks and redemption checks are prepared from this information.

Sale Procedures

The sequence of the published list will be followed as closely as practical during the Tax Lien Sale. There will be a listing of property tax liens to be sold in sequence index number and schedule number order provided to each buyer on sale day.

Each parcel will be offered in compliance with Title 39, Article 11, of the Colorado Revised Statutes. To facilitate the sale procedure, parcels which are contiguous or contained within one subdivision may be combined and sold as a unit. Each parcel or unit will be subject to open floor (general) bidding and will be sold to the buyer who shall further pay the largest amount in excess of said taxes, penalty interest, advertising, and other charges as provided by law. Bonus bids (premiums) will be not less than $1.00 and after reaching a premium of $5.00 will be increased by increments of $5.00 The auctioning will provide all buyers with the opportunity to compete for each parcel or unit.

It is the buyers' responsibility to know the quality of the property on which they are paying the taxes and receiving a lien. The sequence index number and the minimal amount of each parcel or unit will be read only once. All successful bids are final (assuming the buyer has sufficient monies on deposit). No changes in, or cancellation of, parcels purchased can be made after the lien is sold.

The sale will be conducted as rapidly as possible, consistent with the objectives of the sale and fairness to all buyers. The day will be utilized entirely, insofar, as possible, with a one-hour lunch break and fifteen-minute breaks both morning and afternoon. If a continuance is necessary, the sale will be reconvened on the succeeding business day. Announcement of adjournment or reconvening will be made at the sale.

A Tax Lien Sale Certificate of Purchase will be issued for each tax or special assessment lien and will be in the statutory form showing the property description, purchase amount, rate of interest, buyer's name, and the date of sale. Certificates will not be issued in a name other than the name of the buyer. If delinquent taxes occur in the future, the certificate holder may endorse the amount of delinquent taxes and lawful charges on his certificate until redemption.

Redemption Interest

Interest begins in October, 1996 and Tax Lien Sale Certificates of Purchase for 1996 will carry the rate of 14% in accordance with Colorado Revised Statutes. Bonus bids (premiums) are not returned.

Prohibited Buyers

No Adams County official or employee may purchase a tax lien at this sale. This also applies to the immediate family or any agent of an Adams County official or employee.

49

General Information

It must be understood that the sale and purchase of the tax or special assessment lien at a tax sale does not, as it might under simple sales and purchase agreements, convey the right of possession, use, improvement of access to said property. The buyer is issued a Tax Lien Sale Certificate of Purchase which is a properly recorded lien.

In the event the lien remains unredeemed, the certificate holder has the right of paying subsequent years' delinquent taxes (sub-taxing). Sub-taxing normally occurs after the first day of July or August each year, as redemption interest accrues only as of that date. Three years from the date of the certificate, if the lien remains unredeemed, the certificate holder may apply for a Treasurer's Deed to the property. To be eligible for a Treasurer's Deed, the certificate holder must make application to the Treasurer. The procedural process requirements normally take a three to six month period of time to accomplish. Extenuation of the time period may occur when there are complex problems related to the property. Deed applications may be made by the certificate holder six calendar months prior to the third anniversary date of the certificate, but the endorsement of the current year's taxes and/or special assessments will not accrue interest until the first day of July or August. When application is made, monies must be deposited to pay all related deed expenses pursuant to law. Prior to deed application all subsequent taxes, special assessment liens, and current taxes must be paid and endorsed on the certificate.

If the lien is redeemed, the certificate holder is entitled to interest on the taxes, penalty interest, advertising, and legal charges which he paid and subsequent endorsement. Liens may be redeemed at any time prior to the issuance of a Treasurer's Deed.

NOTE

Redemption interest for 1996 Tax Lien Sale Certificates of Purchase will be at the rate of 14% per annum. Portions of a month shall be counted as whole months pursuant to law.

WRONGFULLY SOLD LIEN

If a lien is wrongfully sold and the County must pay the certificate holder the accrued interest, the rate will be 8% per annum for the delinquent tax liens sold this year.

HELEN L. HILL, ADAMS COUNTY TREASURER
If there are further questions, please call: Tax Lien Sales at 654-6165.

IS ALL THIS TOO MUCH WORK?

Is all this requiring more effort on your part than your 2.88% Certificates of Deposit? You betcha! Is it worth the extra amount of trouble? If you don't think so you should stop reading right now and give the book to some who needs the money.

You may invest in Tax Lien Certificates all your life and never acquire a piece of real estate. On the other hand you may *"Win the Lottery"* on your first investment.

If you always invest with the goal of receiving an exceptionally high rate of return on your ***totally secured*** investment. Anything else is just a bonus.

Of course you can put all your money in the stock market. For several years someone took the stock picks of the "experts" and matched them against a monkey throwing a dart at the stock listings in the *Wall Street Journal*.

I don't want to discourage you, but most years the real monkey won.

You gotta do this!

Jim Yocom

Chapter 5

WHAT HAPPENS AT THE AUCTION? EXACTLY!

The greatest mistake you can make in life is to be continually fearing you will make one.

—Elbert Hubbard

I know I am starting to sound like a broken record, but counties are very different in the methods they use to conduct their auctions. You already know that. Now you are going to see some of these differences.

Please don't ever assume that you know what is going to happen at a particular auction just because you are familiar with the procedures in a neighboring county. Check with the County Treasurer for the rules.

Illustration 2 is from a listing of delinquent real estate taxes in Adams County, Colorado. This will give you a good introduction to the kinds of instructions you can expect.

I chose this one because the instructions are pretty clear, as far as they go. After we discuss this letter I will illustrate to you the absolute necessity of studying all the procedures and guidelines before the sale.

HERE IS HOW IT IS DONE IN ONE COUNTY

Look at *Illustration 2*. You will see that date, time and location of the sale is shown first.

The next section tells you how the county will get paid. Adams County requires the money to be on deposit prior to the sale. You will notice that there is one location for making deposits on sale day, and another location if the deposits are made any day prior to the sale.

Adams County will accept personal checks only if guaranteed by an irrevocable letter of credit from your bank. This requires a good relationship with your bank, but it is probably the easiest way to handle your transactions at the sale.

Next you will find that no matter who you are, or how much money you bring; if you want a seat you may need to get there early. These are public auctions. Everyone has an equal chance.

The county requires you to complete a Buyer Data Form and it is very important that you do this accurately. Once this is completed and they have verified that you have funds on deposit you get a bidder number and a card.

Most counties give you about the same kind of card you would get at a furniture auction or a cattle auction. It is often a card with your registration number mounted on a small stick. In open bidding you hold up your card to indicate your bid just as you would in almost any other type of auction.

Illustration 3 is a page from the book showing the listings. The certificates on these properties are auctioned in the same order as the listings.

Bear in mind that you will get an updated list when you arrive at the auction that will be different than the one in this advance publication. This is because the book is published or sent out on disk 30 days in advance of the sale and some of the taxes are paid during this 30 day period.

Take a look at that page. You will see a certificate will be offered for as little as $30 and as much as $62,452.11. I keep insisting that *anyone can invest in Tax Lien Certificates.* Here's the proof.

Remember the story in the first chapter about the conversation with a broker and your *"ridiculous"* demands? Here is how you do what you told the broker: If you add up the total assessed value of all the properties on that page it is $1,147,400. You could buy all the Tax Lien Certificates for $130,777. Where else can you get a first lien on over a million dollars of real estate for $130,000?

Let me answer that. Nowhere.

Oh, I didn't mention the best part. The $1,147,500 is *assessed value* the Fair Market Value is around ten times greater. Is this secured enough?

You gotta do this!

The interest rate set by the State Legislature in Colorado is 9% plus whatever the federal discount rate is on September, 1 of each year. In most years this is from 13% to 14%.

If the federal discount rate is 3% then the interest paid on Tax Lien Certificates would be 12%. This rate will continue until paid even though rates will change in subsequent years. Now it is 2002 and the interest rate is lower because the discount rate is lower.

Colorado uses what is referred to as a "Premium" bidding system. This means the buyers bid on how much more they will pay for the Tax Lien Certificate than the amount of taxes that are due and listed in the publication.

In our example the interest rate remains at 12%. The interest rate is applied to the amount shown to be delinquent. *No interest is paid on the premium.* Tuck this bit of information away for now, we will talk about it a little later.

For example the first property in the second column of *illustration 3* has taxes due in the amount of $820.90. The bidding will start at this amount. The second bidder could raise that amount by one dollar to $821.90. The next bidder could add another dollar over the last bid until the premium reaches $5, then each succeeding bid must be in $5 increments.

Does this mean that you will always have to pay more than the amount of the taxes? No. Not everyone bids on each property. Yours may be the only bid, in which case you will get the Tax Lien Certificate for the amount of the taxes. At most auctions there are a lot more certificates offered than there are investors.

Earlier we said that buying left over certificates over the counter by mail might be your best bet? If you buy this way these certificates are not subject to competitive bidding. You never have to pay a premium.

Remember the information we told you to tuck away? Here's what happens. The interest rate remains constant and is applied to the amount shown in the publication, which will be the opening bid. So every dollar you bid above this amount reduces the yield on your investment.

You should identify the property you want to bid on. Determine the maximum amount you will bid for that certificate. Then stick to your guns. It is easy to get caught up in any auction and pay more than you should. This is true in a Tax Lien Certificate auction also.

Always identify several properties you would like to bid on and have the amount you will bid determined before the auction. Then if you are not successful bidding on the first property you want, you already know your next move.

Look under the section **Sale Procedures in** *illustration 2* at the last sentence, "If delinquent taxes occur in the future, the certificate holder may endorse the amount of delinquent taxes and lawful charges on his certificate until redemption."

As you know when you buy a certificate you are paying all the delinquent taxes as of the purchase date. If the certificate is not redeemed, new taxes are due the following year. You will have the opportunity to pay the new taxes and add them to the amount of the certificate you already own.

This is great! The new taxes are not subject to competitive bidding so you get the maximum interest. And guess what? This certificate is one year closer to the time when the property could be yours.

You are still going to get paid on all your investment.

WHAT IF YOU DON'T PAY SUBSEQUENT TAXES?

If you don't pay the taxes there will be a new certificate issued to someone else. If this new purchaser forecloses because the property owner never pays the taxes, the foreclosure will wipe out your lien.

In the **General Information** section of *illustration 2* you learn that if the taxes aren't paid after a three year redemption period you have the right to apply for a Treasurer's Deed.

All parties with an interest in the property will be notified by the Treasurer and as stated after three to six months have passed you will be issued a deed.

We told you previously that no actual foreclosure is required in Colorado.

Finally, you learn that if the Tax Lien Certificate was sold by mistake the county will pay you 8% interest on your investment. Even the mistakes pay almost twice what your bank pays.

SO THAT'S HOW ONE COUNTY DOES IT.

(WAIT, THERE IS MORE TO THE STORY.)

I told you I would illustrate the absolute necessity of learning how a particular auction works. I told you that the rules of the sale don't tell the entire story.

Here are a couple of things you didn't learn by reading the instructions. It is your responsibility to learn these additional details. The county can't take the time to advise you of every detail unless you ask questions. An important objective of this book is to give you the knowledge to ask the correct questions.

An important thing to be aware of in Colorado, because it uses premium bidding, the premiums are retained by the county. When the property owner pays the taxes owed they do not pay this premium amount. This is why the premium reduces your net yield.

What happens if you pay a premium in order to purchase a certain Tax Lien Certificate and the property owner comes in a few days later and pays the taxes due?

Remember, he doesn't pay the premium. You have only owned the certificate for a few days so the amount of interest you have earned is almost nothing.

The county will send you a check for the amount of your investment, less the premium, and those few days interest but nothing for the premium paid. You would lose whatever amount you paid as a premium.

Premium bidding doesn't always work the way it does in Colorado. Sometimes it is a very good thing. There are states where the surplus earns interest and goes back to the investor if the property is redeemed. Georgia is an example.

Assume that the property owner redeems on the last day of the year in this example.

The total amount due from owner	$5,000
The interest rate is 20%	
Investor bids $5,000 plus $3,000 surplus in order to buy the certificate. Total bid	$8,000
When property owner redeems he must pay	
20% on the total amount of bid -	$1,600
plus taxes and expenses due	$5,000

Total amount paid by property owner $6,600

Investor gets his $5,000 back plus 20% X $5,000 or $1,000 in interest plus 20% earned on the $3,000 surplus: $600 then the state refunds the $3,000 surplus bid.

The property owner has received 20% interest on the total investment. One caveat: if the property owner doesn't redeem, the county retains the surplus. Of course, the investor has the property.

This doesn't happen everywhere. For example, in Iowa you earn 2% per month. The 2% penalty is assessed at the beginning of the month, so even if the taxes are paid the day after the purchase of a Tax Lien Certificate the property owner pays 2% interest for one day. I didn't calculate the rate of return, but it is a lot.

Again, don't panic. This example of the possibility of losing money is in Colorado. Not every state is like this. If you don't like the way they pay in one state just buy in another state.

You can protect yourself by spreading the amount of money you have to invest over several certificates. Not all of them are going to pay off right away, even in Colorado.

Another way to protect yourself is to just not buy if you have to pay more than a few dollars premium. That's why we said to determine the most you will pay for a certificate. Get the yield you want.

You have learned if you purchase over the counter after the sale, there is no competitive bidding; so no premium.

This is why you are reading this book before you invest.

HERE IS A STRATEGY!

Since we are talking about Colorado, here is something else to watch for. Colorado uses a rotational bidding process. It operates, as the name implies, by rotation. Number 1 bids first, then it goes to number 2 to bid or pass, and so on around the room.

If you are at an auction with a lot of people you may not get to bid as often as you would like. There is something you can do to increase your play.

You can register to bid. Then your spouse can register. You can also register a corporation you own, a trust, or any other legal entity. Each will be assigned a number and will get a regular turn in the rotation.

Of course each entity will need to make a deposit in its own name. Later, you can sell all of the certificates you buy into whichever entity is most advantageous for you.

Jim Yocom

Chapter 6

MORE THAN ONE WAY TO BID

Don't wait till your ship comes in; swim out to it.

—Anonymous

You have seen how a tax lien auction works in one county. I have shown you the first bidding procedure; premium bidding. As you have come to expect by now there are other methods.

In Colorado you **bid up** the amount you are willing to pay for a Tax Lien Certificate. In some other states, Indiana, Illinois, New Jersey and Florida, for example, you **bid down** the interest rate.

Lets look at Florida where the interest rate is 18%. The successful bidder is the one who is willing to accept the least amount of interest.

All bids start at 18%. The first bidder will bid 18%. The next bidder might bid 17.75% and the next one 17.5%. This continues until the person willing to accept the smallest interest rate becomes the successful bidder and owns the certificate.

Don't despair and start thinking you can't get the highest return. One person told me about attending a recent auction in Florida. There were in excess of 5,000 Tax Lien Certificates to be sold in that particular county. There were less than 70 people registered to bid so most of the liens sold that day went for the opening bid of 18%. I am told that the majority of the certificates went unsold.

Now that you are learning how this works, guess what happens to the difference between the 18% interest rate the property owner must pay as a penalty, and the interest rate an investor might pay for the certificate?

That was too easy, wasn't it? Of course, the county keeps the difference. Okay, that's fair. (May as well be, that's the way it is.) The investor still got an investment that is *totally secured at a return just not available anywhere else.*

What if the auction was really well attended and the bidding was very competitive? What if the investor had to accept an interest rate of *only 15%?* Dust off that Rule of 72 you learned earlier and you will see that the investors money will double in less than 5 years *while being* **TOTALLY SECURED!**

Check your bank's CD rate or the government bond market for that deal. See what mutual funds have done recently.

Excuse me for continuing to highlight the ***totally secured*** aspect of an investment in Tax Lien Certificates. You just aren't going to lose if you do your homework.

You know from the beginning what your rate of return will be. You can get almost any rate you want, so don't accept anything that you don't want.

You are in control!

You can't compare Tax Lien Certificates to any other investment that is ***not totally secured.*** This eliminates the stock market, including mutual funds. But, you will find that you can easily out perform 99% of the mutual funds, which are not secured, with Tax Lien Certificates that are *TOTALLY SECURED!*

What if the investor invested only $2,000 per year in a self directed IRA for 20 years at 15%? My calculator says there would be over $200,000 in the account at the end of 20 years.

If he didn't put anymore in the IRA after the 20 years, in only four more years and nine months it would grow to $400,000. It would double again in another four years and nine months.

Bear in mind the interest goes to 18% in Florida, so how much would be in this account at the end of 20 years. **$293,255!**

What if this investor invested in Iowa and got 24%. How about Texas where the rate is 25% for just <u>six months</u>? (Texas is a story all by itself. More about that later.)

Do you get the point I'm trying to make? If there is something you don't like about the way one state or county sells Tax Lien Certificates, just buy somewhere else.

YOU GUESSED IT. THERE IS STILL ANOTHER WAY TO BID
(Didn't you just know it?)

In Iowa the rate is 24% per year. They pay 2% per month, or any part of a month. It is one of the best states in which to purchase Tax Lien Certificates.

When a certificate is redeemed (They almost always are. Just as in other states.) You receive your investment plus the 2% per month. The difference in bidding is relevant in the event of foreclosure.

In Iowa you bid on an undivided interest in the property. The person willing to take the smallest percentage is the successful bidder. If you bid the property down to 50% and you foreclose you would own only 50% of the property.

In 99% of the cases this means nothing because the property owner redeems before foreclosure.

I constantly talk to people who get hung up on these foreclosure procedures. Don't. Most people will buy Tax Lien Certificates all their lives and never get involved in actually acquiring the deed to the property. If you do, you are going to make a lot of money even if you only own 50% of a piece of property.

The thing to keep in mind is that you are still making 24%!

Chapter 7

WHAT HAVE YOU LEARNED SO FAR?

The greatest discovery of my generation is that a human being can alter his life by altering his attitude of mind.

—William James

This book is a training manual. It is not something to be read once then set aside like a novel. My goal is to really give you enough knowledge to begin earning the high interest rates that are available to you.

Because it is a training manual you will find certain things repeated. This is just to make sure that you really learn them.

With that thought in mind, let's review.

So far we know that most of the operating revenue for a county comes from revenues received from assessing taxes on real estate. This is called an *ad valorem tax* because it is assessed on the value of the property. This includes all types of property; raw land, agriculture, commercial, industrial, and both single and multi family residential property.

The County Tax Assessor assesses a value to real estate then multiplies that value by a predetermined *county constant* to arrive at an *assessed value*. The assessor then multiplies this assessed value by a *county constant* and the product of this formula becomes the amount of taxes the property owner must pay.

If the property owner does not pay promptly this causes a shortfall in the operating revenue required to fund the operations of the county.

The county has the right to either collect the taxes or seize the property. However, this does not happen immediately. The state legislature sets a redemption period during which property owners can bring their taxes current without losing their property. This happens in around 98% of the cases across the country.

This redemption period varies from state to state. It ranges from six months to as long as five years.

The counties cannot wait as long as five years to receive their operating revenue. About half the counties in the U. S. look to private investors to provide the funds. They do this by creating a Tax Lien Certificate.

This is a certificate that evidences the delinquent taxes owed by the owner of a piece of real estate. This document also gives the owner of this certificate all the same rights the county has.

State legislatures establish a penalty that must be collected by the county against delinquent taxpayers. This penalty is in the form of a rate of interest that must be paid on the amount of delinquent taxes. The penalties range from 8% to as much as 50%.

The counties sell these certificates to private investors at public auctions. Most counties hold auctions annually. Some others may hold several auctions during the course of the year. These are public auctions and anyone can attend and anyone can bid except employees of the county conducting the auction. The certificates range in value from as little as $10 to hundreds of thousands of dollars.

There is an opportunity for everyone to invest in Tax Lien Certificates.

AT THE AUCTION...

Most of the auctions are conducted pretty much the same as any other auction that you may have attended whether the merchandise is fine art, cattle or Jackie Onasis' personal belongings. There are some exceptions in individual counties but this is how it typically goes.

You register for the auction prior to the start and you are assigned a bidding number. This number is printed on a card and you simply hold up the card when you bid.

There are three primary ways that bids are made. Different states have different rules. As you have come to expect there are some slight variations.

BIDDING PROCEDURE NUMBER 1

You bid down the interest rate. As an example Arizona has an 18% rate and the successful bidder is the one that will accept the lowest interest rate.

BIDDING PROCEDURE NUMBER 2

Some states, Colorado, for example, have premium bidding. The certificate is sold to the buyer who pays the largest amount in excess of the taxes, penalty interest, advertising and any other charges provided by law.

BIDDING PROCEDURE NUMBER 3

In this procedure the competitive bidding is for whoever is willing to accept the smallest undivided interest in the property in the event of a foreclosure. This does not effect the interest rate if the certificate is paid off. Remember, they are almost always paid and you collect the interest rate.

The following table will give you more information on the bidding procedure in different states.

Bidding Procedures by State

ALABAMA

Alabama is a *bid up* state. You bid on the total amount due and the successful bidder is the one who bids the most over the amount due. Alabama is one of those states where the surplus goes back to the bidder at redemption. If property is not redeemed the county keeps the surplus.

ARIZONA

In Arizona you *bid down* the interest rate and the one willing to accept the lowest rate is the buyer.

COLORADO

Colorado is a *bid up* state. You bid up the amount to pay over the total amount of taxes and expenses due. Largest premium bidder is the buyer. The county keeps the surplus and the property owner pays no interest on the surplus.

FLORIDA

In Florida you *bid down* the interest rate you will accept

GEORGIA

Georgia is a *bid up* state. If the property is redeemed the investor gets the premium refunded by the county. In the event of foreclosure the county keeps the surplus.

ILLINOIS

Illinois is a *bid down* state.

INDIANA

Indiana is a *bid up* state. Surplus goes to investor at redemption. It is kept by county if foreclosed.

IOWA

Iowa is a state where you bid on an *undivided interest.* The successful bidder is the one who accepts the smallest percentage of undivided interest in the property. You become a joint owner with the property owner.

KENTUCKY

Kentucky presents still another way to bid. Their Tax Lien Certificates are sold by *lottery.* If more than one person wants to buy a lien there is a lottery held on the spot to select the buyer.

LOUISIANA

Louisiana is another state where you bid on an *undivided interest.*

MARYLAND

A *bid up* state. One quirk; the excess bid is sold on credit if you want.

MASSACHUSETTS
Massachusetts in an ***undivided interest*** state.

MISSOURI
Missouri is a ***bid up*** state. Surplus goes back to investor if redeemed.

NEBRASKA
Nebraska is an ***undivided interest*** state.

NEW HAMPSHIRE
New Hampshire is an ***undivided interest*** state.

NEW JERSEY
New Jersey is a ***bid down*** state.

NEW YORK
Check individual counties. New York is a challenge.

NORTH DAKOTA
North Dakota is a ***bid down*** state.

OKLAHOMA
Oklahoma is another ***lottery*** state

SOUTH DAKOTA
South Dakota is a ***bid down*** state

WEST VIRGINIA
West Virginia is a ***bid up*** state. The surplus goes to the investor at redemption but the surplus does not earn interest.

WYOMING

Wyoming is a *lottery state* when your number is drawn you buy or pass.

Is this all you need to know? No. You need to get all the information avaible from any county that you want to invest in. If every piece of information was included in this book it would go to several volumes. But don't let that intimidate you. You will probably never buy in all 3,000 plus counties. Just become an expert where you invest.

YOU BID SUCCESSFULLY—YOU BOUGHT IT!
(Now what?)

Okay, you have attended the auction, raised your card at the appropriate time, your bid was the winning one and you are the proud owner of a Tax Lien Certificate.

What happens next?

First, you will pay for your investment according to the procedures in that particular county. Then within a few days the county will mail the certificate to you.

There are some states who keep the certificate only in their computer and just give you a receipt showing that you have paid for it.

Some time during the redemption period the property owner is probably going to come to the county tax office and bring the taxes current. The county employee will collect all the money due. They collect the taxes, all expenses and the penalty interest due.

If they have mailed you the certificate they will advise you that the taxes have been paid and ask you to surrender the certificate.

The certificate is an important document and should be filed in a safe, fireproof place along with such other papers as the deed to your home, and your insurance policies.

If it is lost most counties make provisions to replace it for you. For example Iowa charges $10 to replace a certificate.

If the county has retained the certificate, usually electronically, all they have to do is mail your check.

WHAT IF YOU CAN'T ATTEND AN AUCTION, OR JUST DON'T WANT TO?

As we discussed this can be the best of all possible ways to buy. Most counties will sell left over Tax Lien Certificates over the counter or by mail after the auction date. There is no competitive bidding and you get the maximum return on your investment. This way of investing is called, "Assignment Purchases."

A lot of investors don't buy any other way. Some counties will sell all the certificates they have at the auction. Another county in the same state won't sell after the auction. This can be because of time constraints or just not enough bidders.

If you want to buy this way just start calling counties in the state where you want to invest until you find one with certificates on hand. Nearly all of them will have certificates for sale.

Here is an exact quote from Yavapai County, Arizona concerning Assignment Purchasing.

"ASSIGNMENTS

"Assignments offer the investor an alternative way to purchase liens on parcels at a time other than the back tax sale.

"The unsold parcels 'struck off to state' at the tax lien sale are available to lien holders by 'Assignments.' The assignment of State CP's begins April, 1 in the Treasurer's office.

"Available parcels are listed in a printout located on the front counter in the Treasurer's office. This printout lists the tax figure, as well as the year involved. The buyer will pay the entire amount of taxes, interest, fees and charges due at the time of assignment. There is an additional $10.00 fee for each assignment.

"NOTE: **If a parcel also has current delinquent taxes in addition to "State CP" taxes, the investor may purchase both after June 1, and prevent the parcel from going to sale in February.**

"ASSIGNMENT PURCHASING

"The buyer will submit a list of desired parcels to the Treasurer's Office, along with a Cashier's Check, Money Order or Certified Check for the approximate total. The submittals will be processed in the order in which they are received.

"The calculations will be made on the assignments up to the amount received. Parcels not covered by funds on hand, must remain available to other buyers.

"Should the original payment be in excess of the amount due, a refund will be issued.

"Be sure to specify "assignment" in order that a redemption is not inadvertently processed. The interest earned on an assignment will be the current statutory maximum (i.e. 16%)"

Pay specific attention to the last paragraph. If you have been concerned about bidding up, bidding down, etc. Here is a simple way, with no competition, to get the maximum interest rate from the comfort of your easy chair. Also, some of these certificates are closer to the redemption date. You may stand a better chance of acquiring property.

But, I did tell you that this was going to take some effort. No one is going to knock on your door with the paperwork all filled out. You have to make the call.

You gotta do this.

...AND IF THEY DON'T PAY?

If the property owner does not pay the taxes during the redemption period you proceed to take title to the property.

How do you do that?

Here comes what must be your favorite phrase by now...*it varies from one county to the other.*

In some states you actually go through a foreclosure procedure. You either hire an attorney to do it for you, or sometimes the county will handle it for you for a fee.

In other states, Colorado for example, you make application to the County Treasurer for a Treasurer's Deed.

One investor bought a Tax Lien Certificate in Colorado on 2.87 acres for $687.50 a couple of years ago. This was not at an auction, but had gone unpurchased and taxes were due since 1993.

As soon as he bought the lien he applied for a Treasurer's Deed because the redemption period had already expired.

He received the deed which wiped out all previous liens. Then he advertised the property on Ebay and sold it for $8,510. He received $2,000 down and is receiving monthly payments on the balance for 48 months.

Just the down payment gave him a 291% return on his $687.50 investment and he has a positive cash flow for four more years.

This is a tough business!

You gotta do this!

Jim Yocom

Chapter 8

WHAT TO WATCH FOR

"I haven't the vaguest idea. I just tell jokes. My lawyers and accountants look into these things and explain them to me in baby talk. If it sounds okay we go ahead."
    —Buddy Hackett on why he invested in a disastrous tax shelter
program

Why do you suppose some people fail to pay their property taxes? Considering the consequences you would think they would never be past due. A penalty of anywhere from 8% to 50% should be enough incentive.

Not only is that not enough for some people, some actually lose their property each year through tax default.

Of course there are lots of reasons. When I was in they Navy they told us that there was always that 1% who just never got the word. I thought that only applied in the military. Not by a country mile.

The point is that sometimes there are just unexplained reasons why property taxes go unpaid.

Sometimes the reasons are obvious. A property owner dies without a will and perhaps no surviving relatives. The property taxes could easily go unpaid. Sometimes the heirs are far away, know little or nothing about the property, and just have no interest in it.

A little imagination and you can come up with all kinds of reasons for unpaid taxes. Some property owners don't pay until the last minute for their own reasons. Maybe they are using this cash to invest in Tax Lien Certificates that earn a higher interest rate than their penalty.

On the downside there are sometimes good reasons why taxes are unpaid. It is possible for a property to become virtually worthless. There can be flood problems, an erosion problem or any problem that will cost more to eliminate than the property is worth.

One thing that comes to mind, and with good reason, is a hazardous waste clean up liability. You remember when our federal government passed the *"Superfund Act."* Like a lot of laws passed by our congress, this one imposes some very harsh burdens on the public.

This law makes the current property owner liable for cleaning up contaminated property. It makes no difference if the property owner was not the one who polluted the property. The present owner could have acquired title today, and the pollution could have occurred twenty years ago. The government in its' infinite wisdom says, "Clean it up! Damn the cost, full speed ahead."

It does no good to discuss the merits, or the lack of them, of this law. You just need to be aware of it and avoid these pitfalls.

How do you avoid this problem? As in most things, there are no guarantees. However, a little thought will probably avoid the problem completely.

Where are you most likely to find a pollution problem? Probably industrial property. This sure doesn't mean that all industrial property is contaminated. It's is just that the use of some industrial property more readily lends itself to the potential for contamination.

Some commercial property can have the same problem. Underground fuel tanks from an old service station site are assumed to be leaking until proven otherwise.

So what can look like a great deal if you own the Tax Lien Certificate on an industrial site may not be such a great deal. If the taxes go unpaid and you become the new owner you could just inherit a mess.

I mentioned earlier that I usually like to buy certificates on residential property. Particularly single family residential property. You are going to be as safe from pollution problems as it is possible to get on this planet.

Even farm land can be declared a marsh land and only good for nesting geese and ducks. Certainly, you don't want to take the chance of owning it.

You might just want to stick to Tax Lien Certificates on residential property.

Are there any other problems to side step? Yes, there are a couple. But before I give you these caveats please allow me to give you one of my own. This book is not intended to render legal or accounting advice. I am not a lawyer. I am going to give you a couple of warnings and solutions.

As I have stressed from the beginning, very few things in this business are consistent. Legalities concerning real estate are another of these inconsistencies. What is perfectly legal in one state does not necessarily hold true in any other state. Always *consult your own lawyer or accountant*.

CIVIL JUDGMENTS & LIENS

If a property owner has been sued in civil court and the person or entity who brought the suit has won a judgment there may be a lien filed against the property owner and everything he or she owns.

This lien can cloud the title on a piece of real estate. The property owner will have to satisfy this judgment in some way and get the lien removed before anyone can get clear title to the property. Which means he probably can't sell it until the lien is cleared.

It is not a problem for you if you foreclose on the property.

This type of lien is junior to a tax lien and will be wiped out by foreclosure. You will own the property free and clear if you do everything properly. Just make sure you consult a lawyer before foreclosing to be sure everything is done correctly.

After the foreclosure you will want to check and make sure that the lien is removed. In all prudence you may want to purchase title insurance and the title company will check on this as part of their research. Once the title company issues a policy it is their responsibility to defend that title and protect you.

In most states title companies will issue a title policy on tax forfeited land after one year if there have been no claims against the property. Others may require a quiet title action. Check with a title company in the area where you may own property, ask them to explain this procedure and their requirements. Check before you own the property.

Until recently one of the hang ups with selling a property such as the one described above was obtaining title insurance quickly. Even though the foreclosure wiped out all the liens some people insist on title insurance.

This can require a quiet title action at some expense and time. Most investors want to sell quickly, realize their profit and buy more Tax Lien Certificates.

Now there is a solution. There is a company that will issue title insurance at a reasonable price on properties such as this for investors.

Contact Dave Schumacher, President
Tax Title Services
(714) 848-4750 FAX (714) 848-8170

TAX LIENS

Tax liens may or may not spell real trouble for you. State and Municipal tax liens are often eliminated through foreclosure by you as the owner of an unredeemed Tax Lien Certificate. If so they are of no great concern. Check with legal counsel in any state where you encounter this situation.

Federal Tax Liens, IRS liens, are another matter altogether. These are the only liens senior to your Tax Lien Certificate in most cases. If you acquire the property you can acquire the lien. This is not a good thing, but it is not necessarily a disaster either. IRS will usually release these liens after foreclosure if you follow their procedure. Check with county officials or directly with the IRS. Make sure you are talking to a senior person at IRS. The person who answers the phone will probably give you the wrong answer.

As I told you I don't do a lot of research. All the problems I am warning you about only apply in that 1% or 2% of the cases where you actually foreclose and acquire the property. An even smaller percentage of the 1% or 2% will have a problem.

You need to do whatever satisfies you. But if I am going to bid on a lien for more than a thousand dollars I want to check for IRS liens. That's usually as far as I go.

DON'T PUT ALL YOUR EGGS IN ONE BASKET.

How often have you heard that? I take it seriously.

I don't like the large dollar amount liens. If I am going to invest $1,000 I would prefer to have 5 liens for $200. If I am investing $10,000 obviously the dollar amount of the lien goes up, but I sure don't want to spread this amount of money over just one or two liens.

I am sharing my personal investment philosophy with you. Again, you will have to develop your own standards for investing in Tax Lien Certificates.

I look at these investments the same way a mutual fund manager looks at the stock market. The idea behind a mutual fund is to both spread the risk and spread the opportunity.

If you buy a single stock you have a 50/50 chance of either making or losing money. In a mutual fund the idea is that if one stock is a loser there are other winners to make up for it. Too bad it doesn't always work like that.

While you certainly don't have the risks of the stock market, things don't necessarily always work the way you would like. Ideally, you purchase a certificate today and the owner does not pay the property taxes until the end of the redemption period. This way you are not having to reinvest that money so often.

But not all of them will pay off quickly. This is the reason to spread your investment over several liens. If one pays off early the rest of your money is still working.

Or you really get lucky and wind up with the property.

Also spreading your money is a lot like playing the lottery. The more tickets you have, the more chances you have to win.

LIQUIDITY

You know before you buy the maximum amount of time you might have to hold a Tax Lien Certificate before you collect your money or the property. Knowing this you do not invest dollars that you may need for emergencies.

Tax Lien Certificates are assignable and can be bought and sold. Don't rely on this if you need immediate cash. There are a handful of companies that will market your Tax Lien Certificate for you for a fee. I am not going to name them because I can't vouch for their integrity.

This is a wealth building vehicle, not a trading vehicle. Their very lack of liquidity is one of the best reasons to invest in them. Since you know you can't get your money out quickly you look elsewhere for ready cash.

Your investment is still working for you long after most emergencies have come and gone.

BANKRUPTCY

Usually a county will catch the fact that there is a bankruptcy and remove a property before the Tax Lien Certificate sale. If they should allow one to slip through they will return your money. Some will even pay you the interest, since it was their fault.

If you are holding a Tax Lien Certificate on a piece of property that is owned by someone who declares bankruptcy after you purchase the lien you need to be cautious.

I said, *"cautious."* I didn't say panicked. Even though bankruptcy procedures will wipe out this individual's debts it does not eliminate your Tax Lien Certificate. You are a **secured** creditor. You are still in the same position. The only thing that can happen is that it may take you longer to sell the property if you should have to foreclose.

But, your Tax Lien Certificate represents 2% or so of the Fair Market Value of the property so waiting isn't so bad with that kind of pay off on the horizon.

Let's see what really happens. First of all read everything you receive from the bankruptcy court. You will need to file a claim. This is done by completing a "Proof of Claim in Bankruptcy" form. If the court doesn't send you one call them to find out where to get one.

This puts everyone on notice of your claim and your position.

The likelihood that you will ever even be faced with the situation is so remote that it barely merits a mention. I just want you to know what to do if it does happen.

NOTICES

In the event you wind up with a piece of property because the owner didn't redeem you need to learn what notices must be given before you foreclose.

Some counties will send notices for you but it is your ultimate responsibility to make sure all proper notices are given. This is why it is wise to hire a *real estate* lawyer to handle the foreclosure for you. An improper notice can void the foreclosure and cause you to lose the property.

It is up to you to know what the different requirements are. Don't leave it to chance. If you are getting the property you want to make sure nothing is left to chance.

Some states require you to start foreclosure at a certain time or you could lose your property.

A question I get a lot is, "What if I wind up with a piece of property that no one wants?" This could happen, particularly if you are buying a lot of liens by mail where you don't have an opportunity to inspect the property.

One investor, using these techniques in this book, wound up with a piece of undeveloped land. When he went to inspect his property he found that it was just a small piece of land next to a Catholic church. It was not large enough to develop so most people had decided that it was worthless.

This investor didn't give up so easily. He had only a couple of hundred dollars invested in the Tax Lien Certificate, expenses and cost of foreclosure. However, the County Assessor had the property assessed at a value of a few thousand dollars.

This investor donated the land to the church. He was allowed to deduct the Fair Market Value, as shown by the

County Assessor, from his taxes. This deduction decreased his taxes, so he made a profit on a piece of *worthless* property.

These are just things to be aware of. Don't let them dampen your enthusiasm.

Just as you look both ways before you cross a street to be safe, you want to be safe in your investments too. Just because safety dictates looking both ways, it doesn't keep you from crossing the street.

Just because I caution you to be prudent doesn't mean you shouldn't invest in Tax Lien Certificates.

Check out the different states and counties until you find the situation you like. I love to live in Colorado, but I usually don't buy Tax Lien Certificates here. There are other states that match my goals much better.

For example, suppose you have determined that you need to earn 18%. Then you automatically rule out all the states listed later that pay less than 18%. Nothing complicated. Maybe you invest in New Jersey because it pays 18%.

What if you want only a six month redemption period? Now you eliminate New Jersey because it has a two year redemption period.

A little reading in this book tells you that Maryland pays 18% and has a six month redemption period.

Sure you are tired of hearing this, but it is just another reminder that you are totally in control.

Where else is this possible? Nowhere. You can switch around in stocks, mutual funds, limited partnerships with nothing but promises and projections or you can stick with something that guarantees that if you don't get paid back your original investment, plus the stated interest, you get the property that secured it. The interest rates don't go down. What a deal! You gotta do this!

Jim Yocom

Chapter 9

OH YES, WE STARTED OUT TALKING ABOUT BECOMING A MILLIONAIRE

Propagandists, from Shakespeare to Jacqueline Susann, have been telling the unrich that money doesn't buy happiness. The unrich, not being immune to spasms of common sense, sometimes wonder about this.

—Anthony Haden-Guest

There are probably as many different reasons for buying this book as there are people who buy it. A lot of people are considering investing in Tax Lien Certificates strictly from an investment perspective. You may invest through a self directed IRA or other retirement program. Great!

Some other people may be considering this as a business. Great!

Maybe you are considering investing as a combination. Great!

My point is, investing in Tax Lien Certificates can satisfy a lot of desires. But nothing happens until you actually ***buy*** a Tax Lien Certificate.

The market is flooded with "How To" books: How to lose weight, How to invest, How to Start a Business, How to Attract a Mate—the list goes on forever.

I would bet that over 90% of these books are read and nothing ever happens. The buyers don't start the diet, the

91

business, or the investments. A lot of the books are bought and never read. I really hope that is not the case with you and this book.

Really! This information eliminates almost any excuse for procrastination that you can think of. You can't say you don't have enough time or knowledge. It takes very little time and you have the knowledge. What's left?

Oh, you don't have the money? Stay with me. I am going to bury that excuse in just a few more pages.

I once heard someone describe the ideal start up business. He said the business would have to meet these five criteria:

1. Cost of initial investment must be less than $1,000
2. The time required could not be more than one hour per week
3. Skill level to start must be zero
4. It must have low risk or no risk
5. The earning potential must be unlimited

I would make the criteria even more demanding with a sixth requirement—***The business must be totally safe. The investment <u>totally secured.</u>*** (I just don't get off that <u>***secured***</u> business, do I?)

Think about what you have learned. Does investing in Tax Lien Certificates meet all six challenges? You bet.

Now think of another secure business that meets all six challenges. Can't think of one? Neither can I.

There are some definite pluses that accrue to you if you are pursuing this as a business. First of all your travel can be tax deductible. Of course you wouldn't want to research tax liens in Florida in the winter time. Would you?

Don't just jump out there and assume you are going to get to deduct your trip to Aunt Nellie's house just because you went to the courthouse and talked to the County Treasurer while you were there. Travel deductions may not be available to the casual investor, but if it is a bona fide business it can be. Check with your CPA.

If you meet the requirements for a home based business you can deduct a portion of your house payments, insurance, taxes, phone bill, utilities, etc. It's a long list. Even if you don't invest in Tax Lien Certificates as a full time business, you need to start some kind of ***legitimate business*** that you run from your home.

Notice how I stressed *legitimate business?* The business has to be set up with the express purpose of making a profit and must be run accordingly. That means keeping accurate records and filing tax returns the same way that other businesses do. Well, except for Enron.

If you don't set up some kind of business think about this. The next time you get in your car drive three miles, roll down your window and throw a dollar out the window. After six miles toss another dollar and keep this up from now on.

This is just one of the things that it is costing you to not have a home based business. That mileage is probably tax deductible if properly documented. It is the last great tax shelter left.

I have a guy mow my lawn once per week. I deduct part of what I pay him. Yes, it is legal if done properly.

You could even buy a computer and deduct the entire cost the first year as a business expense. Make sure you have a good accountant to guide you. But, you don't want one who is afraid to fight for your legitimate deductions.

The accountant's attitude should be, after careful consideration and research, *when in doubt deduct it.* He needs to be the kind who goes into the bull ring with the ketchup already on his sword.

I just feel that all those dollars serve me, and the government for that matter, much better by being invested in Tax Lien Certificates than purchasing $600 toilet seats for government airplanes.

ENDLESS POSSIBILITIES

There are so many ways to take advantage of the high rate of interest you now have at your fingertips. For example, after you have filled all of your tax sheltered investments with Tax Lien Certificates you will want to continue to invest.

Now is the time to become close friends with your banker. You can make great use of financial leverage. It's really simple. You borrow from your bank and invest in Tax Lien Certificates.

There are some restrictions on borrowing to invest and there are really good reasons why. Ordinarily this is a terrible idea. But since this is a **totally secured** investment it could make great sense. You pay your banker whatever rate of interest you negotiate, then invest at a higher rate.

For example, if you pay your banker 12% and buy tax liens in Iowa that pay 24% you are, in essence, earning 12% on the *bank's money.* Talk about role reversal!

Same thing with your credit cards. You can use your credit card at some auctions, but if you can't just get a cash advance. Your monthly payment is going to roughly be the amount of the advance divided by 48 months on most cards. This isn't exact, but it is a good rule of thumb.

If you buy liens on property with short redemption periods that also have an interest rate greater than what your card company is charging it can be another worthwhile leverage.

Of course the bank and credit card company techniques are only good if you can afford the monthly payments. You also have to consider where you would be if you just took the amount you will have to pay the credit card company or bank and invested that amount.

You will probably only want to consider these alternatives if you think you have a reasonable chance of acquiring a desirable property.

Think long and hard before you borrow money. I am just illustrating another option that can be useful in the correct situation.

YOU MAY BE DRIVING A $250,000 AUTOMOBILE

That sounds like an outrageous statement, doesn't it? Walk with me just a couple more steps.

Let's make some quick assumptions. Let's assume you are driving a car with payments of $300 per month. That will describe the majority of Americans.

Now assume that you just paid off the loan. What is the first thing that most people do? That's right they trade for a new car and start all over. Well, that's not really true. Most people trade before the loan is paid off. If that wasn't enough, now we are being sold on leasing which guarantees that we will <u>always</u> be making payments.

I don't want to be held personally responsible for wrecking the Great American Economic Machine. Therefore I am not going to suggest that you stop buying cars whenever you want.

Here is something to consider though. What if just this once, then never again, you go for an entire year <u>*without a car payment*</u>. That's right, just wait 12 months for the new car.

But don't stop making the $300 per month payments. Just make the payments to yourself rather than the bank. Trust me, they won't go broke, especially now that they ***charge you to put money in the bank.***

Take the $3,600 you saved and buy, you guessed it, Tax Lien Certificates. If you bought Iowa certificates your $3,600 would be worth $265,910 in twenty years.

All this for just driving the same car for an extra year. If you keep making car payments and don't invest you have lost out on over a quarter of a million dollars that could have been yours.

We could show the same example with that 60" billion megawatt TV that will keep you in front of it rather than researching another investment.

I know you have to have it. Just wait one year. They will be better and bigger by then anyway.

It's your choice.

BROWN BAG LUNCHES AND POP FROM THE FRIDGE CAN MAKE YOU RICH!

Okay, I can hear the negative nannies saying, "That's fine for people who buy late model or new cars and have $300 payments. I drive really old cars. I can't do this."

I promised you before that I would show you how everyone can afford to do this, to some degree. Here is how.

People tell me all the time that they just don't have any spare money at all. They just can't afford to do anything. I have yet to find anyone who couldn't come up with something if they really looked, provided they are working.

I find that a lot of people who have no money buy their lunch every day. Even at a fast food hamburger joint that has to cost at least $3.00 every day. That's $15 per week or $780 per year.

What if you bring your lunch from home? You can do that for half of what the hamburger and drink costs, so you can save $390 per year.

How many of these people stop at a convenience store and get a "Big Whateveritis" once a day for $1.25 or more per day? A lot, if not most. Or maybe it is a Krispy Kreme. If they bought their drinks at the grocery store and brought them with them they could save $.75 per day which is $3.75 per week or $195 per year.

Add that to the $390 and they are up to $585 per year. Not all the money in the world, but what if just this small amount was invested in Iowa Tax Lien Certificates for 20 years in a Self Directed IRA?

**That's a whopping $177,606!!** _**All this for a brown bag sandwich and canned soda pop.**_

It gets better. At the end of the 20 years they can cash in enough Tax Lien Certificates to pay themselves 24% per year on the $177,606. _**That's $42,625 per year or $3,552 per month.**_

This is from someone who was positive that they had absolutely no money. If that is you, and you don't do this, just think that those $3.00 lunches and huge drinks are actually costing you over $150 per day in future income. I hope they are really good.

Could you actually do this? Tell me just one, even semi valid, reason why not. Sure, your circumstances are probably different. _Which probably means you could invest five times this amount._ Five times this amount would only require you to invest $2,925 per year and it would grow to $888,000 in 20 years.

Go back and look at the first page of Chapter 1 of this book. Now do you believe anyone can become a "Cash Money" millionaire? Why not?

One more thing; how long could you draw the $3,552 per month shown in our first example? In the illustration you are only drawing the interest so you could draw it for as long as you live, as long as your children live, as long as your grandchildren live, in fact forever, and never touch the $177,606 principal.

Now do you agree with Einstein that compound interest is the greatest power on earth?

I can't resist. What do you think these figures would be at 50% interest? You figure it. It is just too outrageous.

You have everything you need. Twenty years is going to pass whether you do anything with this knowledge or not. You determine your own destiny.

Think about it.

Okay, enough is enough. You must surely be convinced by now that you can't just read this book and put it on the shelf.

You really can't afford to not get started. Take a thousand dollars, take a hundred dollars, take twenty five bucks but take something and attend an auction or call around and find a county that has some left over Tax Lien Certificates. Just get started now. ***Please!***

These are new concepts to you. If you have been an investor in the past it may still be hard to imagine that investments that have a 50% yield have been around for over a hundred years and you haven't heard of them. But don't let your old notions keep you from enjoying the returns that are just waiting for you.

I know it takes a paradigm shift for most people. They remind me of the ***Monkey's Fist*** story.

I am told that one of the ways they capture monkeys in the jungle is to build a cage. No, the cage isn't meant to put the monkeys in. The cage is small and the bars are just far enough apart for the monkey to get their hands inside. Inside the cage they put a favorite treat of the monkeys. When the monkey reaches inside and gets the treat in his fist it is too large to get back out of the cage. As the story goes the monkey will hold on to that treat even as they are being captured rather than let go and escape.

A lot of people are like the monkey. They are holding on to their old preconceived ideas so tightly that they just can't let go and enjoy a much better way.

Fortunately, you don't have to let go until you are sure this is for real. Do yourself the biggest favor of your life. Check it out. ___NOW!___ Don't wait another day. Go to your nearest county courthouse and look at the Tax Lien Certificates that are available. Look through some of the record books and start to get familiar with how to do research. Just do it!

No, no, no, don't tell me you will wait until you have some money. We have already put that to rest. Pack the brown bag and spend a day at the courthouse.

You gotta do this.

Chapter 10

HIGH INTEREST IS JUST GREAT, BUT I WANT THE PROPERTY!

If no one wants to make you a star, you might as well do it yourself!

—Mickey Rooney to Judy Garland

Do you want to get an exceptionally high return on your investment, and increase your odds of getting the property? Here's a way to accomplish both. You can not only increase your odds of getting the property you can increase the yield on your investment dramatically.

Go to a state that assesses the penalty in full, immediately. A great example is Texas. Technically Texas is not a Tax Lien Certificate state. Texas sells something very similar called a Tax Deed Certificate. When you buy this you are actually buying the property for the taxes due, but the owner has one more chance to redeem the property before you can make it yours.

You will not find Texas in your directory at the end of the book because it is not a certificate state.

Texas assesses a penalty of 25% that is in full force and effect immediately. If the property owner redeems the property the day after you buy the certificate you still earn

101

25% on the full amount of the certificate even though you have only owned it for one day. This gives you something in the neighborhood of several thousand percent annualized return on your investment.

The property owner only has six months to redeem the property before you can start foreclosure procedures. The six month period means that the least annualized return you will receive is 50%. You are still ***totally secured.***

Try this for a return on Wall Street!

Now you have met your first criteria, you have an extremely high return. Let's see how to maximize it.

As soon as you buy the certificate write a letter to the property owner. Tell the owner that you have purchased a Tax Deed Certificate and he is in imminent danger of losing the property. Explain that you will begin the process of taking possession of the property as soon as possible. Encourage the owner to pay the taxes as soon as possible to avoid the risk of losing the property.

The sooner they pay the greater the return on your investment.

Since there is only a six month redemption period you stand a much greater chance of getting the property. Even if you don't, look at the return. Also you are entitled to collect rent if the property owner is using or occupying the property.

There are other ways to increase your chance of obtaining properties through investments in Tax Lien Certificates.Using the principles that you are learning right now, an investor bought several Tax Lien Certificates in Oklahoma on vacant land. You will remember that Oklahoma only assesses an interest rate of 8%.

But this investor wasn't concerned about the 8%, even though it is about three times what the bank pays. This investor wanted the land.

Did his plan work? Oh yes. He received Tax Deeds on 26% of the Tax Lien Certificates he had purchased.

Remember the earlier story about the fellow who wound up with the acreage in Colorado and sold it on Ebay for a great profit?

GEORGIA ON YOUR MIND
(Or maybe it should be.)

Georgia offers something similar to the situation found in Texas. They have a one year redemption. The interest rate is 20% and is due in full on the first day of the year. If the owner redeems on the first day of the second year the investor has earned 40% in one year and one day.

It gets better. If the investor has to have a notice of foreclosure served by the Sheriff this adds another 20% so an investor can earn 60% in just a very short period of time.

Most of the time you will get the property in both Texas and Georgia, but if you only earn 50% or 60%, it ain't bad.

Jim Yocom

Chapter 10

NOW YOU KNOW HOW, HERE IS WHERE

Nothing in the world can take the place of perseverance. Talent will not: nothing is more common than unsuccessful men with talent. Genius will not: unrewarded genius is almost a proverb. Education alone will not: the world is full of educated derelicts. Persistence and determination alone are omnipotent.

—Calvin Coolidge

Hopefully by now you are convinced that this is not rocket science. It is really very simple. It is not much more difficult than opening one of those wonderful 2.88% savings accounts.

What follows is a listing of most of the counties in the United States that sell Tax Lien Certificates and a place to make notes. There are some cities that sell them, Baltimore for example, but the great majority of certificates are sold by counties.

There is a state page that gives general information about rates, redemption periods, etc. Behind each state page is the county listings.

A few words before you get into this directory. This will always be a work in progress. County offices move from one office to another, they change phone numbers, and sometimes they change addresses altogether. It is

105

impossible to have every one up to date at any given moment.

I am sharing this with you so you don't get frustrated if you dial a number that has been changed. Even area codes are changing rapidly. I have two area codes in my house. You will occasionally find an address that is outdated. I have tried to obtain the latest information but I would have to do a daily update in order to keep it current. Don't allow a minor frustration stop you. Just call information and keep going. Many numbers are for the county switchboard, just ask for the Treasurer's Office.

Have a secure, even wealthy future. You have the tools.
___You gotta do this___*! You really do!*

ALABAMA

**Alabama has a statutory penalty interest rate of 12%
There is a three year redemption period. At the end
of three years you can request, and receive a Tax Deed
At the auction you bid up the sale price.**

ALABAMA

BALDWIN
(205) 937-0245
PO Box 1549
Bay Minette, AL

BUTLER
(205) 382-3221
PO Box 756
Greenville, AL

CALHOUN
(205) 237-1911
1702 Noble Street
Anninston, AL

CHEROKEE
(205) 927-5527
Cherokee County Courthouse
Ceutre, AL

CHOCTAW
(205) 459-2411
117 South Mulberry Street
Butler, AL

CLARK
(205) 275-3377
PO Box 9
Grove Hill, AL

CLAY
(205) 275-3377
PO Box 155
Ashland, AL

CLEBURNE
(205) 463-2873
406 Vickery Street
Heflin, AL

COFFEE
(205) 347-8734
100 S. Edwards St.
Enterprise, AL

COLBERT
(205) 386-8538
PO Box 1236
Tuseuwbia, AL

COOSA
(205) 377-4916
PO Box 7
Rockford, AL

CRENSHAW
(205) 335-6568
PO Box 208
Luverne, AL

CULLMAN
(205) 739-3535
PO Box 220
Cullman, AL

DALE
(205) 774-2226
Dale County Courthouse
Ozark, AL

DALLAS
(205) 874-2519
105 Lauderdale St.
Selvia, AL

ELMORE
(205) 567-1118
PO Box 396
Wetumpka, AL

FRANKLIN
(205) 332-8841
PO Box 248
Russellville, AL

GENEVA
(205) 684-3119
PO Box 326
Geneva, AL

GREENE
(205) 372-3144
PO Box 45
Eutaw, AL

JACKSON
(205) 574-9390
PO Box 307
Scottsboro, AL

JEFERSON
(205) 325-5500
Hefferson County Courthouse
Birmingham, AL

LAUDERDALE
(205) 760-5785
PO Box 794
Florence, AL

LIMESTONE
(205) 233-6435
Limestone County Courthouse
Athens, AL

MACON
(205) 724-2603
101 E. Northside
Tuskeege, AL

MARENGO
(205)295-2214
Marengo County Courtehouse
Linden, AL

MOBILE
(205) 690-8530
PO Box 7
Mobile, AL

PICKENS
(205) 367-2040
PO Box 447
Carrollton, AL

PIKE
(205) 566-1792
Pike County Courthouse
Troy, AL

RUSSELL
(205) 298-6661
PO Box 669
Phenix City, AL

ST. CLAIR
(205) 594-5143
PO Box 1129
Ashville, AL

SUMTER
(205) 652-2251
PO Box DD
Livingston, AL

TUSCALOOSA
(205) 359-3870
Tuscaloosa County Courthouse
Greensboro, AL

ARIZONA

**Arizona has a statutory penalty interest rate of 16%
Sale dates are in February and vary by county
Bid down the interest rate. Certificate going to person willing to Accept the lowest interest rate.
You can purchase by mail with no bidding down after the tax sale**

ARIZONA

APACHE
(520) 337-4364
PO Box 669
St. Johns, AZ 89536

COCHISE
(520) 432-9322
PO Box 1778
Bisbee, AZ 85603

COCONINO
(520) 779-6615
100 East Birch Street
Flagstaff, AZ 86001

GRAHAM
(520) 428-3440
800 Main Street
Safford, AZ 85546

GILA
(520) 425-3231
1400 East Ash Street
Globe, AZ 85501

GREENLEE
(520) 865-3422
PO Box 1227
Clifton, AZ 85533

LA PAZ
(520) 669-6145
PO Box B Q
Parker, AZ 85344

MARICOPA
(620) 506-8511
301 West Jefferson
Phoenix, AZ 85003

MOHAVE
(520) 753-0737
PO Box 712
Kingman, AZ 86401

NAVAJO
(520) 524-4172
PO Box 668
Holbrook, AZ 86025

PIMA
(520) 740-8344
110 West Congress
Tucson, AZ 85701

PINAL
(520) 868-6425
PO Box 729
Florence, AZ 85232

SANTA CRUZ
(520) 761-7800
Nogales, AZ 85628

YAVAPAI
(520) 771-3233
255 East Gurley
Prescott, AZ 86301

YUMA
(520) 329-2048
Yuma, AZ 85364

COLORADO

Colorado has a statutory penalty interest rate of 9% plus the Federal Discount Rate on September 1st of the year of the sale. The rate then remains consistent throughout the year for new sales. Tax Lien Certificates will continue to accrue interest at the rate set at the time of purchase. New purchases will carry the new interest rate.

Sale dates vary by county

COLORADO

ADAMS
(303) 654-6165
450 S. 4th
Brighton, CO 80601

ARAPAHOE
(303)795-4950
5334 Prince St.
Littleton, CO 80166

ARCHULETA
(303) 264-2152
PO Box 148
Pagosa Springs, CO 81147

BACA
(719) 741 Main Street
Springfield, CO 81073

BOULDER
(303) 441-3520
1777 6th Street
Boulder, CO 80306

CHAFFEE
(719) 539-6808
132 Crestone
Salida, CO 81201

CHEYENNE
(719) 767-5657
51 South First Street
Cheyenne Wells, CO 80810

CLEAR CREEK
(303) 569-3251
PO Box 2000
Georgetown, CO 80444

CONEJOS
(719) 376-5919
PO Box 127
Conejos, CO 81129

CASTILLA
(719) 672-3342
PO Box 100
San Luis, CO 81151

CROWLEY
(719) 267-4624
6th and Main Street
Ordway, CO 81063

CUSTER
(719) 783-2341
205 South 6th Street
Westcliffe, CO 81252

DELTA
(303) 874-2135
501 Palmer
Delta, CO 81416

DELORES
(303) 677-2386
PO Box 614
Dove Creek, CO 81324

DOUGLAS
(303)660-7455
301 South Wilcox Street
Castle Rock, CO 80104

EAGLE
(303) 328-8860
PO Box 597
Eagle, CO 81631

ELBERT
(303) 621-3120
751 Ute Street
Kiowa, CO 80117

EL PASO
(719) 520-6666
20 East Vermijo Street
Colorado Springs, CO 80903

GARFIELD
(303) 945-6382
109 8th Street
Glenwood Springs, CO 81601

GILPIN
(303) 582-5222
203 Eureka Street
Central City, CO 80247

GRAND
(303) 725-3347
PO Box 192
Hot Sulphur Springs, CO 80451

GUNNISON
(303) 641-2231
200 E. Virginia Ave.
Gunnison, CO 81230

HUERFANO
(719) 738-1280
400 Main Street
Walsenburg, CO 81089

JACKSON
(303) 723-4220
PO Box 337
Walden, CO 81089

JEFFERSON
(303) 271-8330
1701 Arapahoe, Street
Golden, CO 80419

KIOWA
(719) 438-5831
PO Box 353
Eads, CO 81036

KIT CARSON
(719) 346-8434
Burlington, CO 80807

LAKE
(719) 486-0530
PO Box 55
Leadville, CO 80461

LA PLATA
(970) 382-6239
PO Box 99
Durango, CO 81302

LARIMER
(970) 498-7020
PO Box 1250
Fort Collins, CO 80522

LAS ANIMAS
(719) 846-2981
Trinidad, CO 81082

LINCOLN
(719) 743-2633
PO Box 67
Hugo, CO 80821

LOGAN
(303) 522-2462
300 Main Street
Sterling, CO 80751

MESA
(303) 244-9183
PO Box 200
Grand Junction, CO 81502

MINERAL
9719) 658-2360
PO Box 70
Creede, CO 81130

MOFFAT
(970) 824-6670
227 West Victory Lane
Craig, CO 81625

MORGAN
(303) 867-5615
PO Box 1289
Montrose, CO 81402

OTERO
(719) 384-5473
13 West Third Street
Lajunta, CO 81050

OURAY
(970) 325-4405
PO Box C
Ouray, CO 81427

PARK
(719) 836-2771
PO Box 220
Fairplay, CO 80440

PITKIN
(303) 925-7635
506 Main Street
Aspen, CO 81611

PHILLIPS
(303) 854-2822
221 S. Interocean Ave.
Holyoke, CO 80734

PROWERS
(719) 336-2081
301 South Main
Lamar, CO 81052

PUEBLO
(719) 583-6000
211 West 10th
Pueblo, CO 81003

RIO BLANCO
(970) 878-3614
PO Box G
Meeker, CO 81641

ROUTT
(303) 879-1732
522 Lincoln Ave.
Steamboat Springs, CO 80477

SAGUACHE
(719) 655-7522
PO Box 356
Saguache, CO 81149

SAN JUAN
(970) 387-5488
PO Box 466
Silverton, CO 81433

SAN MIGUEL
(303) 728-3891
PO Box 919
Telluride, CO 81435

SEDGWICK
(303) 474-3627
PO Box 3
Julesburg, CO 80737

SUMMIT
(303) 453-2561
PO Box 868
Breckenridge, CO 80424

TELLER
(719) 689-2574
PO Box 959
Cripple Creek, CO 80720

WASHINGTON
(303) 345-2756
150 Ash Strteet
Akron, CO 80720

WELD
(303) 356-4000
915 10th Ave.
Greeley, CO 80631

YUMA
(303) 332-5809
310 Ash
Wray, CO 80758

FLORIDA

Florida has a statutory penalty interest rate of 18%
Sales dates can vary by county and from year to year
At the auction the interest rate is bid down in ¼%
increments the successful bidder is the one accepting the
lowest interest rate

A $1,000 deposit is required and purchases are
charged against this amount. Any money left over is
returned within 30 days. If you purchase more than the
deposit you can pay 10% down and the balance
according to county requirements.

The redemption period is 22 months. After 22
months an unpaid certificate holder can apply for a Tax
Deed.

FLORIDA

ALACHUA
(904) 374-5236
201 East University
Gainsville, FL 32602

BAKER
(904) 259-6880
55 North Third Street
Macclenny, FL 32063

BAY
(850) 235-2285
300 E. Fourth Street
Panama City, FL 32402

BRADFORD
(904) 964-6044
945 N. Temple Ave.
Starke, FL 32091

BREVARD
(407) 264-5283
700 S. Park Ave.
Titusville, FL 32781

BROWARD
(305) 468-3433
115 S. Andrews Ave.
Fort Lauderdale, FL 33301

CALHOUN
(850) 674-4545
425 E. Central Ave.
Blounstown, FL 32424

CHARLOTTE
(813) 743-1354
116 W. Olympia
Punta Gorda, FL 33950

CITRUS
(904) 637-9485
Inverness Hwy 41
Inverness, FL 32650

CLAY
(904) 269-6302
825 N. Orange Ave.
Green Cove Springs, FL 32043

COLLIER
(813) 774-8171
3301 Tamiami Trail
Naples, FL 33962

COLUMBIA
(904) 758-1080
145 N. Hernando St.
Lake City, FL32056

DADE
(305) 375-1790
111 NW First Street
Miami, FL 331`28

DeSOTO
(813) 993-4861
201 E. Oak St.
Arcadia, FL 33821

DIXIE
(904) 498-1213
351 King Street
Cross City, FL 32628

DUVAL
(904) 630-2059
330 E. Bay St.
Jacksonville, FL 32202

ESCAMBIA
(904) 436-5714
223 S. Pala Fox Place
Pensacola, FL 32501

FLAGER
(904) 437-7408
200 East Moody
Bunnell, FL 32010

FRANKLIN
(904) 653-8861
PO Box 340
Apalachicola, FL 32320

GADSDEN
(904) 627-7255
10 E. Jefferson
Quincy, FL 32351

GILCHRIST
(904) 463-3170
112 S. Main St.
Trenton, FL 32693

GLADES
(813) 946-0626
500 Ave. J
Moore Haven, FL 33471

GULF
(850) 639-5068
100 5th Street
Port Saint Joe, FL 32456

HAMILTON
(904) 792-1284
207 NE 1st Street
Jasper, FL 32052

HARDEE
(813) 773-4174
417 E. Main St.
Wauchula, FL 33873

HENDRY
(813) 675-5205
PO Box 1760
LaBelle, FL 33935

HERNANCO
(904) 754-4180
20 N. Main St.
Brooksville, FL 34601

HIGHLANDS
(941) 386-6565
430 S. Commerce
Sebring, FL 33781

HILLSBOROUGH
(813) 272-6000
419 Pierce St.
Tampa, FL 33601

HOLMES
(904) 547-1116
201 N. Oklahoma St.
Bonifay, FL 32425

INDIAN RIVER
(407) 567-8000
2864 Madison St.
Vero Beach, FL 32960

JACKSON
(904) 482-9653
4445 Lafayette St.
Marianna, FL 32446

JEFFERSON
(904) 342-0148
1240 N. Jefferson St.
Monticello, FL 32344

LAFAYETTE
(904) 294-1961
County Court House
Mayo, FL 32066

LAKE
(904) 343-9622
315 West Main St.
Tavares, FL 32773

LEE
(813) 335-2317
2115 2nd Street
Fort Myers, FL 33901

LEON
(904) 488-4381
301 South Monroe
Talahassee, FL 32302

LEVY
(904) 486-5174
355 South Court Street
Bronson, FL 32621

LIBERTY
(904) 643-2442
PO Box 400
Bristol, FL 32321

MADISON
(904) 973-6136
112 E. Pickney
Madison, FL 32340

MANATEE
(813) 741-4820
1115 Manatee Ave. W
Bradenton, FL 33506

MARION
(904) 288-5746
110 NW 1st Ave.
Cala, FL 34475

MARTIN
(407) 288-5746
100 East Ocean Blvd.
Stuart, FL 33494

MONROE
(305) 294-8403
500 Whitehead St.
Key West, FL 33040

NASSAU
(904) 261-5566
416 Center St.
Fernandina Beach, FL 32034

OKALOOSA
(904) 689-5700
101 E. James Lee Blvd
Crestview, FL 32536

OKEECHOBE
(813) 763-3421
304 NW 2nd St.
Okeechobee, FL 33472

ORANGE
(407) 836-2700
46 E. Robinson St.
Orlando, FL 32801

OSCEOLA
(407) 847-1421
12 S. Vernon St.
Kissimee, FL 32741

PALM BEACH
(407) 35502266
301 N. Olive
West Palm Beach, FL 33401

PASEO
(904) 521-4408
705 E. Live Oak Ave.
Dade City, FL 38053

PINELLAS
(813) 363-3561
315 Court Street
Clearwater, FL 34616

PUTMAN
(904) 329-0272
410 St. James Ave.
Palatka, FL 32078

SAINT JOHNS
(904) 823-2250
244 S. Matanzas Blvd.
St. Augustine, FL 32085

SAINT LUCIE
(407) 462-1650
221 S. Indian River Dr.
Ft. Pierce, FL 33450

SANTA ROSA
(904) 623-0135
801 Caroline SE
Milton, Fl 32570

SARASOTA
(813) 951-5620
2000 Main St.
Sarasota, FL 34237

SEMINOLE
(407) 321-1130
300 North Park Ave.
Sanford, FL 32771

SUMTER
(904) 793-0260
209 N. Florida St.
Bushnell, FL 33513

SUWANNEE
(904) 364-3440
200 South Ohio Ave.
Live Oak, FL 32060

TAYLOR
(904) 838-3517
108 N. Jefferson
Perry, FL 32347

UNION
(904) 496-3331
55 Main St. W
Lake Butler, FL 32054

VOLUSIA
(904) 736-5939
120 W. Indiana Ave.
DeLand, FL 32720

WAKULLA
(904) 926-3371
202 Oklochnee St.
Crawfordville, FL32326

WALTON
(904) 898-8121
100 East Nelson
DeFuniak Springs, FL 32434

WASHINGTON
(904) 638-6276
203 W. Cypress
Chipley, FL 32428

ILLINOIS

Illinois has a statutory penalty interest rate of 18% each six months

The successful bidder is the one willing to accept the lowest rate of interest.

The redemption period is three years for most properties. Check each county.

Sale dates vary by county.

ILLINOIS

ALEXANDER COUNTY
County Courthouse
2000 Washington Avenue
Cairo, IL 62914-1717
Phone: (618) 734-0386

BOND COUNTY
County Courthouse
200 W. College
Greenville, IL 62246-0407
Phone: (618) 664-1966

BOONE COUNTY
County Courthouse
601 North Main Street
Belvidere, IL 61008-2708
Phone: (815) 547-4770

BROWN COUNTY
County Courthouse
1 Court Street, Room 4
Mount Sterling, IL 62353-0142
Phone: (217) 773-3421

BUREAU COUNTY
County Courthouse
700 S. Main Street
Princeton, IL 61356-0366
Phone: (815) 875-2014

CALHOUN COUNTY
County Courthouse
P.O. Box 187
Hardin, IL 62047-0187
Phone: (618) 576-2351

CASS COUNTY
County Courthouse
100 East Springfield Street
Virginia, IL 62691
Phone: (217) 452-7217

CHAMPAIGN COUNTY
County Courthouse
101 E. Main
Urbana, IL 61801
Phone: (217) 384-3772

CLARK COUNTY
Christian County
County Courthouse
P.O. Box 647
TAYLORVILLE, IL
Phone: (217) 824-4969

CLAY COUNTY
County Courthouse
P.O. Box 160
Louisville, IL 62858-0160
Phone: (618) 665-3626

CLINTON COUNTY
County Courthouse
PO Box 308
Carlyle, IL 62231
Phone: (618) 594-2464

CRAWFORD COUNTY
County Courthouse
P.O. Box 602
Robinson, IL 62454-0602
Phone: (618) 546-1212

CUMBERLAND COUNTY
County Courthouse
P.O. Box 146
Toledo, IL 62468-0146
Phone: (217) 849-2631

DE WITT COUNTY
County Courthouse
P.O. Box 439
Clinton, IL 61727-0439
Phone: (217) 935-2119

DOUGLAS COUNTY
County Courthouse
P.O. Box 467
Tuscola, IL 61953
Phone: (217) 253-2411

EDGAR COUNTY
County Courthouse
115 West Court Street
Paris, IL 61944
Phone: (217) 466-7433

EDWARDS COUNTY
County Courthouse
50 E. Main Street
Albion, IL 62806
Phone: (618) 445-2115

FAYETTE COUNTY
County Courthouse
PO Box 5004
Vandalia, IL 62471
Phone: (618) 283-5000

FRANKLIN COUNTY
County Courthouse
P.O. Box 607
Benton, IL 62812
Phone: (618) 438-3221

FULTON COUNTY
County Courthouse
PO Box 226
Lewistown, IL 61542
Phone: (309) 547-3041

GALLATIN COUNTY
County Courthouse
P.O. Box 550
Shawneetown, IL 62984-0550
Phone: (618) 269-3025

GREENE COUNTY
County Courthouse
519 North Main
Carrollton, IL 62016
Phone: (217) 942-5443

GRUNDY COUNTY
County Administration Center
1320 Union Street
Morris, IL 60450
Phone: (815) 941-3400

HAMILTON COUNTY
County Courthouse
McLeansboro, IL 62859
Phone: (618) 643-2721

HANCOCK COUNTY
County Courthouse
P.O. Box 39
Carthage, IL 62321-0039

HARDIN COUNTY
County Courthouse
P.O. Box 187
Elizabethtown, IL 62931

Phone: (618) 287-2251

HENDERSON COUNTY
County Courthouse
P.O. Box 308
Oquawka, IL 61469-0308
Phone: (309) 867-2911

JASPER COUNTY
County Courthouse
100 West Jordan Street
Newton, IL 62448-1973
Phone: (618) 783-3124

JEFFERSON COUNTY
County Courthouse
Mount Vernon, IL 62864
Phone: (618) 244-8000

JERSEY COUNTY
County Courthouse
102 West Pearl Street
Jerseyville, IL 62052-1675
Phone: (618) 498-5571

JO DAVIES COUNTY
County Courthouse
330 North Bench Street
Galena, IL 61036
Phone: (815) 777-0161

JOHNSON COUNTY
County Courthouse
P.O. Box 96
Vienna, IL 62995-0096
Phone: (618) 658-3611

KENDALL COUNTY
County Office Building
111 W. Fox Street
Yorkville, IL 60560-1675
Phone: (630) 553-4183

KNOX COUNTY
County Courthouse
200 South Cherry Street
Galesburg, IL 61401-4912
Phone: (309) 343-3121

LA SALLE COUNTY
County Courthouse
707 E Etna Road
Ottawa, IL 61350-1047
Phone: (815) 434-8200

LAWRENCE COUNTY
County Courthouse
1100 State Street
Lawrence, IL 62439
Phone: (618) 943-2346

LIVINGSTON COUNTY
County Courthouse
112 W. Madison Street
Pontiac, IL 61764
Phone: (815) 844-2006

MACOUPIN COUNTY
County Courthouse
P.O. Box 39
Carlinville, IL 62626-0039
Phone: (217) 854-3214

MARION COUNTY
County Courthouse
P.O. Box 637
Salem, IL 62881-0637
Phone: (618) 548-3400

MARSHALL COUNTY
County Courthouse
PO Box 328
Lacon, IL 61540-0328
Phone: (309) 246-6325

MASON COUNTY
County Courthouse
P.O. Box 77
Havana, IL 62644-0077
Phone: (309) 543-6661

MASSAC COUNTY
County Courthouse
P.O. Box 429
Metropolis, IL 62960-0429
Phone: (618) 524-5213

MCDONOUGH COUNTY
County Courthouse
1 Courthouse Square
Macomb, IL 61455
Phone: (309) 837-2308

MENARD COUNTY
County Courthouse
PO Box 456
Petersburg, IL 62675-0456
Phone: (217) 632-2415

MERCER COUNTY
County Courthouse
100 SE 3rd Street
Aledo, IL 61231
Phone: (309) 582-7021

MONROE COUNTY
County Courthouse
100 S. Main Street
Waterloo, IL 62298-1322
Phone: (618) 939-8681

MONTGOMERY COUNTY
County Courthouse
1 Courthouse Square
Hillsboro, IL 62049
Phone: (217) 532-9530

MORGAN COUNTY
County Courthouse
300 W. State Street
Jacksonville, IL 62650-2083
Phone: (217) 245-4619

MOULTRIE COUNTY
County Courthouse
10 South Main Street
Sullivan, IL 61951
Phone: (217) 728-4389

PERRY COUNTY
County Courthouse
P.O. Box 438, Route 127 S.
Pinckneyville, IL 62274-0438
Phone: (618) 357-5116

PIKE COUNTY
County Courthouse
100 East Washington Street
Pittsfield, IL 62363
Phone: (217) 285-6812

POPE COUNTY
County Courthouse
400 Main Street
Golconda, IL 62938
Phone: (618) 683-4466

PULASKI COUNTY
County Courthouse
P.O. Box 218
Mound City, IL 62963-0218
Phone: (618) 748-9360

PUTNAM COUNTY
County Courthouse
P.O. Box 13
Hennepin, IL 61327
Phone: (815) 925-7129

RANDOLPH COUNTY
County Courthouse
1 Taylor Street
Chester, IL 62233
Phone: (618) 826-2510

RICHLAND COUNTY
County Courthouse
103 W. Main
Olney, IL 62450
Phone: (618) 392-3111

SALINE COUNTY
County Courthouse
10 East Poplar Street
Harrisburg, IL 62946
Phone: (618) 252-6905

SCHUYLER COUNTY
County Courthouse
Rural Route 1, PO Box 43E
Rushville, IL 62681
Phone: (217) 322-4734

SCOTT COUNTY
County Courthouse
23 East Market Street
Winchester, IL 62694
Phone: (217) 742-3178

SHELBY COUNTY
County Courthouse
PO Box 230
Shelbyville, IL 62565
Phone: (217) 774-4421

ST. CLAIR COUNTY
County Courthouse
10 Public Square
Belleville, IL 62220-1623
Phone: (618) 277-6600

STARK COUNTY
County Courthouse
P.O. Box 97
Toulon, IL 61483-0097
Phone: (309) 286-5911

STEPHENSON COUNTY
county courthouse
15 North Galena Avenue
Freeport, IL 61032-4348
Phone: (815) 235-8289

TAZEWELL COUNTY
McKenzie Building
Fourth And Court Streets
Pekin, IL 61554
Phone: (309) 477-2272

UNION COUNTY
County Courthouse
P.O. Box H
Jonesboro, IL 62952-0478
Phone: (618) 833-5711

WABASH COUNTY
County Courthouse
P.O. Box 277
Mount Carmel, IL 62863-0277
Phone: (618) 262-4561

WARREN COUNTY
County Courthouse
100 W. Broadway
Monmouth, IL 61462
Phone: (309) 734-8592

WASHINGTON COUNTY
County Courthouse
101 E. St. Louis Street
Nashville, IL 62263
Phone: (618) 327-8314

WAYNE COUNTY
County Courthouse
P.O. Box 187
Fairfield, IL 62837-0187
Phone: (618) 842-5182

WHITE COUNTY
County Courthouse
P.O. Box 339
Carmi, IL 62821-0339
Phone: (618) 382-7211

WILLIAMSON COUNTY
County Courthouse
200 West Jefferson
Marion, IL 62959-3061
Phone: (618) 997-1301

WINNEBAGO COUNTY
County Courthouse
404 Elm Street
Rockford, IL 61101-1212
Phone: (815) 987-2590

WOODFORD COUNTY
County Courthouse
115 N. Main Street, Suite 202
Eureka, IL 61530-1274
Phone: (309) 467-2822

INDIANA

Indiana has an unusual method of accruing interest on Tax Lien Certificates. The rate is 10% for the first six months. Then the rate increases to 15% for the next six months. After one year he rate increases to 25% and remains until redemption or foreclosure.

Interest rate is bid down

Sale dates vary by county.

INDIANA

ADAMS COUNTY
County Courthouse
112 South Second
Decatur, IN 46733-1618
Phone: (219) 724-2600

BARTHOLOMEW COUNTY
County Courthouse
440 3rd St.
Columbus, IN 47201

BENTON COUNTY
County Courthouse
706 East 5th Street
Fowler, IN 47944-1556
Phone: (765) 884-0930

BLACKFORD COUNTY
County Courthouse
110 West Washington
Hartford City, IN 47348
Phone: (765) 348-1620

BOONE COUNTY
201 Courthouse Square
Lebanon, IN 46052-2126
Phone: (765) 482-2940

BROWN COUNTY
P.O. Box 37
Nashville, IN 47448-0037
Phone: (812) 988-5485

CARROLL COUNTY
P.O. Box 28
Delphi, IN 46923-0028
Phone: (317) 564-3172

CASS COUNTY
200 Court Park
Logansport, IN 46947
Phone: (219) 753-7720

CLARK COUNTY
City-County Bldg, 501 E. Court
Jeffersonville, IN 47130
Phone: (812) 283-4451

CLINTON COUNTY
125 Courthouse Square
Frankfort, IN 46041
Phone: (765) 659-6330

CRAWFORD
PO Box 316
English, IN 47118
Phone: (812) 338-2601

DAVIESS COUNTY
200 East Walnut
Washington, IN 47501
Phone: (812) 254-8662

DEARBORN COUNTY
County Administration Bldg.
215 West High Street
Lawrenceburg, IN 47025-1662
Phone: (812) 537-8824

DEKALB COUNTY
County Courthouse
100 South Main Street
Auburn, IN 46706
Phone: (219) 925-2362

DELAWARE COUNTY
County Courthouse
100 West Main Street
Muncie, IN 47305
Phone: (765) 747-7726

DUBOIS COUNTY
1 Courthouse Square
Jasper, IN 47546
Phone: (812) 481-7000

FAYETTE COUNTY
County Courthouse
401 Central Avenue
Connersville, IN 47331-1903

Phone: (765) 825-8987

FLOYD COUNTY
City County Building
311 West 1st
New Albany, IN 47150
Phone: (812) 948-5466

FOUNTAIN COUNTY
301 4th Street
Covington, IN 47932
Phone: (765) 793-2243

FRANKLIN COUNTY
County Courthouse
459 Main Street
Brookville, IN 47012-1405
Phone: (765) 647-4631

FULTON COUNTY
815 Main Street
Rochester, IN 46975-1546
Phone: (219) 223-2912

GIBSON COUNTY
County Courthouse
101 N. Main
Princeton, IN 47670-0168
Phone: (812) 385-4927

GRANT COUNTY
County Courthouse
Marion, IN 46953
Phone: (765) 668-8871

GREENE COUNTY
County Courthouse
Bloomfield, IN 47424
Phone: (812) 384-8532

HAMILTON COUNTY
County Courthouse
One Hamilton County Square
Noblesville, IN 46060
Phone: (317) 776-9601

HANCOCK COUNTY
County Courthouse
9 E. Main, Room 208
Greenfield, IN 46140
Phone: (317) 462-1106

HARRISON COUNTY
County Courthouse
300 N. Capitol Ave.
Corydon, IN 47112
Phone: (812) 738-8241

HENDRICKS COUNTY
P.O. Box 599
Danville, IN 46122-0188
Phone: (317) 745-9221

HENRY COUNTY
County Courthouse
101 S. Main
New Castle, IN 47362
Phone: (765) 529-6401

HOWARD COUNTY
117 N. Main
Kokomo, IN 46901
Phone: (765) 456-2216

HUNTINGTON COUNTY
County Courthouse
201 N. Jefferson, Room 103
Huntington, IN 46750
Phone: (219) 358-4822

JACKSON COUNTY
P. O. Box 122
Brownstown, IN 47220
Phone: (812) 358-6116

JASPER COUNTY
County Courthouse
Box 5
Rensselaer, IN 47978
Phone: (219) 866-4930

JAY COUNTY
County Courthouse
120 Court Street

Portland, IN 47371
Phone: (219) 726-7575

JEFFERSON COUNTY
County Courthouse
300 E. Main Street
Madison, IN 47250-3537
Phone: (812) 265-8921

JENNINGS COUNTY
P.O. Box 383
Vernon, IN 47282
Phone: (812) 346-2131

JOHNSON COUNTY
5 West Jefferson
Franklin, IN 46131
Phone: (317) 736-5000

KNOX COUNTY
Vincennes, IN 47591-2022
Phone: (812) 885-2502

LA PORTE COUNTY
813 Lincolnway
La Porte, IN 46350
Phone: (219) 326-6808

LAGRANGE COUNTY
105 North Detroit Street
LaGrange, IN 46761
Phone: (219) 463-3442

LAKE COUNTY
2293 N Main Street
Crown Point, IN 46307-1854
Phone: (219) 755-3200

MADISON COUNTY
16 E. 9th Street
Anderson, IN 46016-1538
Phone: (765) 641-9470

MARION COUNTY
2500 City-County Building
Indianapolis, IN 46204
Phone: (317) 236-3200

MARSHALL COUNTY
112 W. Jefferson Street
Plymouth, IN 46563
Phone: (219) 935-8555

MARTIN COUNTY
P.O. Box 600
Shoals, IN 47581-0600
Phone: (812) 247-3731

MIAMI COUNTY
PO Box 184
Peru, IN 46970-2231
Phone: (765) 472-3901

MONROE COUNTY
County Courthouse
Bloomington, IN 47402-0547
Phone: (812) 349-2550

MONTGOMERY COUNTY
P.O. Box 768
Crawfordsville, IN 47933-0768
Phone: (765) 364-6430

MORGAN COUNTY
180 S. Main St.
Martinsville, IN 46151
Phone: (765) 342-1001

NEWTON COUNTY
201 North Third Street
Kentland, IN 47951-0143
Phone: (219) 474-6081

NOBLE COUNTY
County Courthouse
101 North Orange Street
Albion, IN 46701-1049
Phone: (219) 636-2658

OHIO COUNTY
413 Main St.
Rising Sun, IN 47040
Phone: (812) 438-2062

ORANGE COUNTY
205 E. Main Street
Paoli, IN 47454
Phone: (812) 723-2649

OWEN COUNTY
60 S Main
Spencer, IN 47460
Phone: (812) 829-5000

PARKE COUNTY
116 West High Street
Rockville, IN 47872-1716
Phone: (765) 569-3422

PERRY COUNTY
County Courthouse
2219 Payne Street
Tell City, IN 47586-2830
Phone: (812) 547-6427

PIKE COUNTY
801 Main Street
Petersburg, IN 47567
Phone: (812) 354-8448

PORTER COUNTY
155 Indiana Avenue
Valparaiso, IN 46383
Phone: (219) 465-3332

POSEY COUNTY
P.O. Box 745
Mount Vernon, IN 47620-0745
Phone: (812) 838-1300

PULASKI COUNTY
112 E. Main
Winamac, IN 46996
Phone: (219) 946-3653

PUTNAM COUNTY
1 West Washington Street
Greencastle, IN 46135
Phone: (765) 653-4603

RANDOLPH COUNTY
100 South Main Street
Winchester, IN 47394
Phone: (765) 584-7070

RIPLEY COUNTY
P.O. Box 235
Versailles, IN 47042
Phone: (812) 689-6115

RUSH COUNTY
101 East 2nd Street
Rushville, IN 46173-1854
Phone: (765) 932-2077

SCOTT COUNTY
1 E. McClain Ave.
Scottsburg, IN 47170-1662
Phone: (812) 752-8408

SHELBY COUNTY
407 S. Harrison Street
Shelbyville, IN 46176
Phone: (317) 392-6330

SPENCER COUNTY
200 Main Street
Rockport, IN 47635-0012
Phone: (812) 649-4376

ST. JOSEPH COUNTY
101 South Main Street
South Bend, IN 46601
Phone: (219) 235-9534

STARKE COUNTY
County Courthouse
53 E. Mound Street
Knox, IN 46534
Phone: (219) 772-9101

STEUBEN COUNTY
County Courthouse
55 S. Public Square
Angola, IN 46703
Phone: (219) 668-1000

SULLIVAN COUNTY
County Courthouse
PO Box 370
Sullivan, IN 47882-0370
Phone: (812) 268-4491

SWITZERLAND COUNTY
County Courthouse
212 West MaIn Street
Vevay, IN 47043
Phone: (812) 427-3302

TIPPECANOE COUNTY
County Courthouse
301 Main Street
Lafayette, IN 47901-1211
Phone: (765) 423-9326

TIPTON COUNTY
County Courthouse
101 East Jefferson
Tipton, IN 46072
Phone: (765) 675-2794

VANDERBURGH COUNTY
County Courthouse
825 Sycamore Street
Evansville, IN 47708-1831
Phone: (812) 435-5241

VERMILLION COUNTY
County Courthouse
P.O. Box 190
Newport, IN 47966-0190
Phone: (765) 492-3570

VIGO COUNTY
Third & Wabash
Terre Haute, IN 47807
Phone: (812) 462-3367

WABASH COUNTY
County Courthouse
1 W. Hill Street
Wabash, IN 46992
Phone: (219) 563-0661

WARREN COUNTY
County Courthouse
125 N Monroe Street
Williamsport, IN 47993-1198
Phone: (765) 762-3275

WARRICK COUNTY
County Courthouse
109 W. Main Street
Boonville, IN 47601
Phone: (812) 897-6120

WASHINGTON COUNTY
County Courthouse
99 Public Square
Salem, IN 47167
Phone: (812) 883-4805

WAYNE COUNTY
301 East Main Street
Richmond, IN 47374
Phone: (765) 973-9200

WELLS COUNTY
105 W Market Street, Suite 205
Bluffton, IN 46714
Phone: (219) 824-6470

WHITE COUNTY
P.O. Box 260
Monticello, IN 47960
Phone: (219) 583-5761

WHITLEY COUNTY
County Courthouse
101 W VanBuren
Columbia City, IN 46725
Phone: (219) 248-3100

IOWA

Iowa is one of the most popular states for investors. Iowa has a statutory penalty interest rate of 24%. This is a great rate byt the yield can be considerably higher because of purchase/redemption dates.

The penalty is charted at the rate of 2% per month *or any part of the month*.

A certificate purchased on the last day of a month and redeemed on the first day of the following month would still earn 2%

Sale dates vary by county

IOWA

ADAIR COUNTY
400 public Square
Greenfield, IA 50849-1259
Phone: (641) 743-2445

ADAMS COUNT
P.O. Box 28
Corning, IA 50841
Phone: (515) 322-3340

ALLAMAKEE COUNTY
110 Allamakee Street
Waukon, IA 52172-1747
Phone: (563) 568-3522

BENTON COUNTY
P.O. Box 549
Vinton, IA 52349-0719
Phone: (319) 472-2365

BOONE COUNTY
201 State Street
Boone, IA 50036
Phone: (515) 433-0502

BUCHANAN COUNTY
P.O. Box 317
Independence, IA 50644-0317
Phone: (319) 334-2196

BUENA VISTA COUNTY
P.O. Box 220
Storm Lake, IA 50588-0220
Phone: (712) 749-2542

BUTLER COUNTY
P.O. Box 325
Allison, IA 50602-0325
Phone: (319) 267-2670

CALHOUN COUNTY
416 4th Street
Rockwell City, IA 50579
Phone: (712) 297-7741

CARROLL COUNTY
P.O. Box 867
Carroll, IA 51401-0867
Phone: (712) 792-4923

CASS COUNTY
5 W. 7th Street
Atlantic, IA 50022-1492
Phone: (712) 243-4570

CEDAR COUNTY
400 Cedar Street
Tipton, IA 52772-1750
Phone: (319) 886-3168

CERRO GORDO COUNTY
220 North Washington
Mason City, IA 50401-3254
Phone: (641) 421-3021

CHEROKEE COUNTY
520 West Main Street
Cherokee, IA 51012
Phone: (712) 225-6704

CHICKASAW COUNTY
P.O. Box 311
New Hampton, IA 50659-0311
Phone: (641) 394-2100

CLARKE COUNTY
100 South Main Street
Osceola, IA 50213
Phone: (614) 342-3311

CLAY COUNTY
215 West 4th Street
Spencer, IA 51301-3822
Phone: (712) 262-1569

CLAYTON COUNTY
P.O. Box 416
Elkader, IA 52043-0416
Phone: (563) 245

CLINTON COUNTY
County Administration Building
1900 North 3rd Street
Clinton, IA 52733
Phone: (563) 244-0560

CRAWFORD COUNTY
1202 Broadway
Denison, IA 51442-0423
Phone: (712) 263-3045

DALLAS COUNTY, IA
801 Court Street
Adel, IA 50003-1476
Phone: (515) 993-5816

DAVIS COUNTY
Courthouse Square
Bloomfield, IA 52537
Phone: (515) 664-2344

DECATUR COUNTY
207 North Main
Leon, IA 50144
Phone: (641) 446-4382

DELAWARE COUNTY
301 East Main Street
Manchester, IA 52057
Phone: (319) 927-2515

DELAWARE COUNTY
301 East Main Street
Manchester, IA 52057
Phone: (319) 927-2515

DICKINSON COUNTY
1802 Hill Avenue
Spirit Lake, IA 51360-1259
Phone: (712) 336-3356

DUBUQUE COUNTY
720 Central
Dubuque, IA 52001
Phone: (319) 589-4441

EMMET COUNTY
609 1st Avenue North
Estherville, IA 51334
Phone: (712) 362-4261

FAYETTE COUNTY
P.O. Box 267
West Union, IA 52175-0267
Phone: (319) 422-3497

FLOYD COUNTY
101 South Main Street
Charles City, IA 50616-2756
Phone: (641) 257-6131

FRANKLIN COUNTY
P.O. Box 26
Hampton, IA 50441-0026
Phone: (641) 456-5622

FREMONT COUNTY
P.O. Box 610
Sidney, IA 51652-0610
Phone: (712) 374-2415

GREENE COUNTY
114 N. Chestnut
Jefferson, IA 50129
Phone: (515) 386-2316

GRUNDY COUNTY
706 G Avenue
Grundy Center, IA 50638
Phone: (319) 824-3122

GUTHRIE COUNTY
200 N 5th
Guthrie Center, IA 50115
Phone: (515) 747-3512

HAMILTON COUNTY
2300 Superior Street
Webster City, IA 50595-3195
Phone: (515) 832-9530

HANCOCK COUNTY
855 State Street
Garner, IA 50438-1637
Phone: (641) 923-3163

HARDIN COUNTY
1215 Edgington Avenue
Eldora, IA 50627
Phone: (641) 858-3461

HARRISON COUNTY
111 North 2nd Avenue
Logan, IA 51546
Phone: (712) 644-2401

HENRY COUNTY
P.O. Box 149
Mount Pleasant, IA 52641-0149
Phone: (319) 385-0759

HOWARD COUNTY
137 North Elm
Cresco, IA 52136-1526
Phone: (319) 547-2880

HUMBOLDT COUNTY
203 Main Street, Box 100
Dakota City, IA 50529-0100
Phone: (515) 332-1571

IDA COUNTY
401 Moorehead Street
Ida Grove, IA 51445-1429
Phone: (712) 364-2626

IOWA COUNTY
P.O. Box 126
Marengo, IA 52301-0126
Phone: (319) 642-3923

JACKSON COUNTY
201 West Platt
Maquoketa, IA 52060-2295
Phone: (563) 652-3144

JASPER COUNTY
P.O. Box 944
Newton, IA 50208
Phone: (641) 792-7016

JEFFERSON COUNTY
P.O. Box 984
Fairfield, IA 52556-0984
Phone: (641) 472-2851

JOHNSON COUNTY
County Administrative Building
913 S. Dubuque
Iowa City, IA 52244
Phone: (319) 356-6000

JONES COUNTY
P.O. Box 109
Anamosa, IA 52205

KEOKUK COUNTY
101 S. Main Street
Sigourney, IA 52591-1499
Phone: (641) 622-2320

KOSSUTH COUNTY
114 West State Street
Algona, IA 50511-2613
Phone: (515) 295-2718

LEE COUNTY
933 Avenue H - P.O. Box 190
Fort Madison, IA 52627
Phone: (319) 372-6557

LOUISA COUNTY
117 South Main
Wapello, IA 52653
Phone: (319) 523-3371

LUCAS COUNTY
916 Braden Avenue
Chariton, IA 50049-1825
Phone: (515) 774-2018

LYON COUNTY
206 S. 2nd Avenue
Rock Rapids, IA 51246
Phone: (712) 472-3713

MADISON COUNTY
P.O. Box 152
Winterset, IA 50273-0152
Phone: (515) 462-3225

MAHASKA COUNTY
106 South 1st Street
Oskaloosa, IA 52577
Phone: (641) 673-3469

MARION COUNTY
P.O. Box 497
Knoxville, IA 50138-0497
Phone: (515) 828-2231

MARSHALL COUNTY
1 East Main Street
Marshalltown, IA 50158
Phone: (641) 754-6330

MILLS COUNTY
418 Sharp Street
Glenwood, IA 51534
Phone: (712) 527-3146

MITCHELL COUNTY
508 State Street
Osage, IA 50461
Phone: (515) 732-5861

MONONA COUNTY
610 Iowa Avenue
Onawa, IA 51040-1660
Phone: (712) 423-1585

MONROE COUNTY
Benton Avenue East
Albia, IA 52531
Phone: (515) 932-7706

MONTGOMERY COUNTY
P.O. Box 469
Red Oak, IA 51566-0469
Phone: (712) 623-5127

MUSCATINE COUNTY
401 East 3rd Street
Muscatine, IA 52761-4168
Phone: (319) 263-5317

O'BRIEN COUNTY
P.O. Box M
Primghar, IA 51245
Phone: (712) 757-3255

OSCEOLA COUNTY
300 7th Street
Sibley, IA 51249
Phone: (712) 754-2241

PAGE COUNTY
112 East Main
Clarinda, IA 51632
Phone: (712) 542-3219

PALO ALTO COUNTY
1010 Broadway
Emmetsburg, IA 50536
Phone: (712) 852-2924

PLYMOUTH COUNTY
215 4th Avenue S.E.
Le Mars, IA 51031
Phone: (712) 546-6100

POCAHONTAS COUNTY
99 Court Square
Pocahontas, IA 50574
Phone: (712) 335-3361

POLK COUNTY
County Administrative Office Bldg.
111 Court Avenue
Des Moines, IA 50309-2218
Phone: (515) 286-3117

POTTAWATTAMIE COUNTY
227 South Sixth Street
Council Bluffs, IA 51501-4208
Phone: (712) 328-5604

POWESHIEK COUNTY
P.O. Box 57
Montezuma, IA 50171
Phone: (641) 623-5443

SCOTT COUNTY
416 West Fourth Street
Davenport, IA 52801-1104
Phone: (563) 326-8611

SHELBY COUNTY
612 Court Street
Harlan, IA 51537-1441
Phone: (712) 755-3831

SIOUX COUNTY
PO Box 18
Orange City, IA 51041-0018
Phone: (712) 737-2216
Fax: (712) 737-2537

STORY COUNTY
900 6th Street
Nevada, IA 50201-2052
Phone: (515) 382-7200

TAMA COUNTY
100 West High Street
Toledo, IA 52342-1333
Phone: (515) 484-3980

TAYLOR COUNTY
405 Jefferson
Bedford, IA 50833
Phone: (712) 523-2280

UNION COUNTY
300 North Pine
Creston, IA 50801
Phone: (515) 782-7918

VAN BUREN COUNTY
P.O. Box 475
Keosauqua, IA 52565-0475
Phone: (319) 293-3129

WAPELLO COUNTY
101 W. Fourth Street
Ottumwa, IA 52501-2510
Phone: (641) 683-0020

WARREN COUNTY
301 North Buxton, Suite 202
Indianola, IA 50125
Phone: (515) 961-1028

WAYNE COUNTY
P.O. Box 435
Corydon, IA 50060-0435
Phone: (515) 872-2221

WEBSTER COUNTY
703 Central Ave
Fort Dodge, IA 50501-3853
Phone: (515) 573-7175

WINNEBAGO COUNTY
126 South Clark Street
Forest City, IA 50436-1706
Phone: (641) 582-3412

WINNESHIEK COUNTY
201 W. Main Street
Decorah, IA 52101-1713
Phone: (319) 382-5085

WOODBURY COUNTY
620 Douglas Street
Sioux City, IA 51101-1248
Phone: (712) 279-6525

WORTH COUNTY
1000 Central Avenue
Northwood, IA 50459-1523
Phone: (341) 324-2316

Jim Yocom

WRIGHT COUNTY
115 North Main
Clarion, IA 50525
Phone: (515) 532-3262

KENTUCKY

Kentucky has a statutory penalty interest rate of 12%

Sale dates vary by county

KENTUCKY

ADAIR COUNTY
424 Public Square
Columbia, KY 42728
Phone: (270) 384-2801

ALLEN COUNTY
P.O. Box 115
Scottsville, KY 42164
Phone: (270) 237-3631

BATH COUNTY
P.O. Box 39
Owingsville, KY 40360-0039
Phone: (606) 674-6346

BOONE COUNTY
2950 Washington Street
Burlington, KY 41005
Phone: (606) 334-2100

BOYD COUNTY
P.O. Box 423
Catlettsburg, KY 41129-0423
Phone: (606) 739-4134

BRACKEN COUNTY
PO Box 264
Brooksville, KY 41004
Phone: (606) 735-2300

BRECKINRIDGE COUNTY
P.O. Box 227
Hardinsburg, KY 40143-0538

BUTLER COUNTY
P.O. Box 626
Morgantown, KY 42261-0626
Phone: (270) 526-3433

CALLOWAY COUNTY
101 South Fifth Street
Murray, KY 42071
Phone: (270) 753-2920

CARLISLE COUNTY
P.O. Box 279
Bardwell, KY 42023-0279
Phone: (270) 628-3233

CHRISTIAN COUNTY
511 South Main Street
Hopkinsville, KY 42240
Phone: (270) 887-4100

CLAY COUNTY
316 Main Street, Suite 129
Manchester, KY 40962
Phone: (606) 598-2071

CRITTENDEN COUNTY
107 South Main Street
Marion, KY 42064
Phone: (270) 965-5251

DAVIESS COUNTY
212 St. Ann Street
Owensboro, KY 42301
Phone: (270) 685-8424

ELLIOTT COUNTY
P.O. Box 710
Sandy Hook, KY 41171
Phone: (606) 738-5421

FAYETTE COUNTY
200 East Main Street
Lexington, KY 40507-1315
Phone: (859) 258-3000

FLOYD COUNTY
P.O. Box 1089
Prestonsburg, KY 41653
Phone: (606) 886-9193

FULTON COUNTY
2204 S. 7th St.
Hickman, KY 42050
Phone: (270) 236-2594

GARRARD COUNTY
15 Public Square
Lancaster, KY 40444
Phone: (606) 792-3531

GRAVES COUNTY
201 E. College Street
Mayfield, KY 42066-2728
Phone: (270) 247-1733

GREEN COUNTY
203 West Court Street
Greensburg, KY 42743
Phone: (270) 932-5386

HANCOCK COUNTY
P.O. Box 580
Hawesville, KY 42348
Phone: (270) 927-8137

HARLAN COUNTY
PO Box 670
Harlan, KY 40831-0670
Phone: (606) 573-2600

HART COUNTY
P.O. Box 409
Munfordville, KY 42765
Phone: (270) 524-5219

HENRY COUNTY
P.O. Box 202
New Castle, KY 40050-0202
Phone: (502) 845-5707

HOPKINS COUNTY
10 South Main Street
Madisonville, KY 42431
Phone: (270) 821-7361

JEFFERSON COUNTY
Louisville, KY 40202-2814
Phone: (502) 574-2273

JOHNSON COUNTY
P.O. Box 868
Paintsville, KY 41240-0868
Phone: (606) 789-2550

KNOTT COUNTY
P.O. Box 1287
Hindman, KY 41822
Phone: (606) 785-5592

LARUE COUNTY
209 W. High Street
Hodgenville, KY 42748
Phone: (270) 358-4400

LAWRENCE COUNTY
122 South Main Cross
Louisa, KY 41230-1700
Phone: (606) 638-4102

LESLIE COUNTY
P.O. Box 619
Hyden, KY 41749
Phone: (606) 672-3200

LEWIS COUNTY
514 2nd Street
Vanceburg, KY 41179
Phone: (606) 796-2722

LIVINGSTON COUNTY
P.O. Box 70
Smithland, KY 42081
Phone: (270) 928-2106

LYON COUNTY
P.O. Box 698
Eddyville, KY 42038-0698
Phone: (270) 388-7311

MAGOFFIN COUNTY
P.O. Box 430
Salyersville, KY 41465-0530
Phone: (606) 349-2313

MARSHALL COUNTY
1101 Main Street
Benton, KY 42025
Phone: (270) 527-4750

MASON COUNTY
219 Stanley Reed Court
Maysville, KY 41056
Phone: (606) 564-6706

MCCREARY COUNTY
P.O. Box 579
Whitley City, KY 42653-0579
Phone: (606) 376-2413

MEADE COUNTY
516 Fairway Drive
Brandenburg, KY 40108
Phone: (270) 422-3967

MERCER COUNTY
134 South Main Street
Harrodsburg, KY 40330
Phone: (606) 734-6310

MONROE COUNTY
P.O. Box 305
Tompkinsville, KY 42167-0305
Phone: (270) 487-5505
Fax: (270) 487-6516

MORGAN COUNTY
450 Prestonsburg Street
West Liberty, KY 41472
Phone: (606) 743-3949

NELSON COUNTY
113 E. Stephen Foster Avenue
Bardstown, KY 40004-1500
Phone: (502) 348-1820

OHIO COUNTY
P.O. Box 146
Hartford, KY 42347
Phone: (270) 298-4400

OWEN COUNTY
P.O. Box 465
Owenton, KY 40359-0465
Phone: (502) 484-3405

PENDLETON COUNTY
233 Main Street, Room 4
Falmouth, KY 41040-0129
Phone: (859) 654-4321

PIKE COUNTY
Pikeville, KY 41501
Phone: (606) 432-6247

PULASKI COUNTY
P.O. Box 712
Somerset, KY 42502-0712
Phone: (606) 678-4853

RUSSELL COUNTY
P.O.Box 397
Jamestown, KY 42629-0397
Phone: (270) 343-2112

SHELBY COUNTY
501 Main Street
Shelbyville, KY 40065-1133
Phone: (502) 633-1220

SPENCER COUNTY
P.O. Box 397
Taylorsville, KY 40071-0397
Phone: (502) 477-3205

TODD COUNTY
P.O. Box 355
Elkton, KY 42220-0355
Phone: (270) 265-2363

TRIMBLE COUNTY
P.O. Box 251
Bedford, KY 40006-0251
Phone: (502) 255-7196

WARREN COUNTY
429 E 10th Street
Bowling Green, KY 42101-2250
Phone: (270) 842-9416

WAYNE COUNTY
109 Main Street
Monticello, KY 42633-0565
Phone: (606) 348-4241

WHITLEY COUNTY
PO Box 237
Williamsburg, KY 40769
Phone: (606) 549-6002

WOODFORD COUNTY
103 South Main Street, Room 200
Versailles, KY 40383
Phone: (859) 873-4139

MARYLAND

Interest rates vary at the discretion of entities offering Tax Lien Certificates from 12% to 24%.
The city of Baltimore has a redemption rate of 24$

MARYLAND

ALLEGANY COUNTY
701 Kelly Road, Suite 405
Cumberland, MD 21502
Phone: (301) 777-5911

ANNE ARUNDEL COUNTY
7 Church Circle
Annapolis, MD 21401
Phone: (410) 222-7000

BALTIMORE COUNTY
400 Washington Avenue
Towson, MD 21204
Phone: (410) 887-3196

CALVERT COUNTY
175 Main Street
Prince Frederick, MD 20678-3337
Phone: (410) 535-1600

CITY OF BALTIMORE
City Hall
100 North Holliday Street
Baltimore, MD 21202
Phone: (410) 396-4892

CAROLINE COUNTY
109 Market Street, Room 109
Denton, MD 21629
Phone: (410) 479-0660

CARROLL COUNTY
225 North Center Street
Westminster, MD 21157-5194
Phone: (410) 386-2400

CECIL COUNTY
129 East Main Street
Elkton, MD 21921
Phone: (410) 996-5201

DORCHESTER COUNTY
206 S. High Street
Cambridge, MD 21613-0026
Phone: (410) 228-6300

FREDERICK COUNTY
12 E. Church Street
Winchester Hall
Frederick, MD 21701
Phone: (301) 694-1100

GARRETT COUNTY
203 South Fourth Street
Oakland, MD 21550-1535
Phone: (301) 334-8970

HARFORD COUNTY
20 West Courtland Street
Bel Air, MD 21014-3745
Phone: (410) 638-3343

HOWARD COUNTY
3430 Courthouse Drive
Ellicott City, MD 21043
Phone: (410) 313-2011

KENT COUNTY
103 North Cross Street
Chestertown, MD 21620
Phone: (410) 778-7435

MONTGOMERY COUNTY
50 Maryland Avenue
Rockville, MD 20850-2540
Phone: (301) 217-7778

PRINCE GEORGE'S COUNTY
14741 Governor Oden Bowie Drive, 3200
Upper Marlboro, MD 20772-3050
Phone: (301) 952-4131

QUEEN ANNE'S COUNTY
107 N. Liberty Street
Centreville, MD 21617
Phone: (410) 758-1773

SOMERSET COUNTY
P.O. Box 37
Princess Anne, MD 21853-0037
Phone: (410) 651-0320

ST. MARY'S COUNTY
P.O. Box 653
Leonardtown, MD 20650-0653
Phone: (301) 475-4461

TALBOT COUNTY
County Courthouse
11 North Washington Street
Easton, MD 21601
Phone: (410) 770-8001

WASHINGTON COUNTY
County Courthouse Annex
100 W. Washington St.
Hagerstown, MD 21740
Phone: (301) 791-3090

WICOMICO COUNTY
P.O. Box 870
Salisbury, MD 21803-0870
Phone: (410) 548-4801

WORCESTER COUNTY
County Courthouse
1 West Market Street
Snow Hill, MD 21863-1072
Phone: (410) 632-1194

MASSACHUSETTS

While Massachusetts is a Tax Lien state the laws are so vague that I am not listing more information about the sales.

If you have good reason to try and buy a tax lien there, contact the local Treasurer's Office for information.

MISSISSIPPI

Penalty interest rates can vary by county in Mississippi.

Generally the rate is 17%.   Contact individual counties.

Sale dates vary by county.

MISSISSIPPI

ADAMS COUNTY
P.O. Box 1008
Natchez, MS 39121-1008
Phone: (601) 442-2431

ALCORN COUNTY
P.O. Box 69
Corinth, MS 38834-0069
Phone: (662) 286-7700

AMITE COUNTY
P.O. Box 680
Liberty, MS 39645
Phone: (601) 657-8022

BENTON COUNTY
P.O. Box 218
Ashland, MS 38603-0218
Phone: (662) 224-6611

BOLIVAR COUNTY
P.O. Box 698
Cleveland, MS 38732
Phone: (662) 843-2071

CALHOUN COUNTY
P.O. Box 8
Pittsboro, MS 38951-0008
Phone: (662) 983-3117

CARROLL COUNTY
1 Pinson Square
Carrollton, MS 38917
Phone: (601) 237-9274

CHICKASAW COUNTY
101 North Jefferson Street
Houston, MS 38851
Phone: (662) 456-2513

CHOCTAW COUNTY
P.O. Box 250
Ackerman, MS 39735-0250
Phone: (662) 285-6329

CLAIBORNE COUNTY
410 Main Street
Port Gibson, MS 39150
Phone: (601) 437-4992

CLARKE COUNTY
P.O. Box 616
Quitman, MS 39355-0616
Phone: (601) 776-3567

CLAY COUNTY
P.O. Box 815
West Point, MS 39773-0815
Phone: (662) 494-3124

COPIAH COUNTY
P.O. Box 551
Hazlehurst, MS 39083
Phone: (601) 892-2994

COVINGTON COUNTY
P.O. Box 1679
Collins, MS 39428-1679
Phone: (601) 765-8605

DE SOTO COUNTY
2535 Highway 51 S.
Hernando, MS 38632-2132
Phone: (662) 429-1460

FRANKLIN COUNTY
P.O. Box 297
Meadville, MS 39653-0297
Phone: (601) 384-2330

GEORGE COUNTY
355 Cox Street, Suite D
Lucedale, MS 39452
Phone: (601) 947-7506

GREENE COUNTY
P.O. Box 460
Leakesville, MS 39451
Phone: (601) 394-2394

GRENADA COUNTY
P.O. Box 1208
Grenada, MS 38902-1208
Phone: (662) 226-1821

HANCOCK COUNTY
P.O. Box 429
Bay Saint Louis, MS 39520
Phone: (228) 467-0172

HARRISON COUNTY
P.O. Box CC
Gulfport, MS 39502-0860
Phone: (228) 865-4001

HINDS COUNTY
P.O. Box 686
Jackson, MS 39205-0686
Phone: (601) 968-6501

HOLMES COUNTY
P.O. Box 239
Lexington, MS 39095-0239
Phone: (662) 834-2508

HUMPHREYS COUNTY
P.O. Box 547
Belzoni, MS 39038-0547
Phone: (662) 247-1740

ISSAQUENA COUNTY
P.O. Box 27
Mayersville, MS 39113
Phone: (662) 873-2761

ITAWAMBA COUNTY
PO Box 776
Fulton, MS 38843
Phone: (662) 862-3421

JACKSON COUNTY
P.O. Box 998
Pascagoula, MS 39568-0998
Phone: (228) 769-3100

JASPER COUNTY
P.O. Box 1047
Bay Springs, MS 39422-1047
Phone: (601) 764-3368

JEFFERSON COUNTY
P.O. Box 145
Fayette, MS 39069-0145
Phone: (601) 786-3021

JEFFERSON DAVIS COUNTY
P.O. Box 1137
Prentiss, MS 39474-1137
Phone: (601) 792-4204

JONES COUNTY
P.O. Box 1468
Laurel, MS 39441-1468
Phone: (601) 428-3139

KEMPER COUNTY
P.O. Box 188
De Kalb, MS 39328-0188
Phone: (601) 743-2460

LAFAYETTE COUNTY
P.O. Box 1240
Oxford, MS 38655-1240
Phone: (662) 234-2131

LAUDERDALE COUNTY
P.O. Box 1587
Meridian, MS 39302-1587
Phone: (601) 482-9746

LAWRENCE COUNTY
P.O. Box 1160
Monticello, MS 39654
Phone: (601) 587-7162

LEAKE COUNTY
P.O. Drawer 72
Carthage, MS 39051-0072
Phone: (601) 267-8002

LEE COUNTY
P.O. Box 1785
Tupelo, MS 38801-1785
Phone: (662) 841-9110

LEFLORE COUNTY
P.O. Box 250
Greenwood, MS 38935-0250
Phone: (662) 455-3904

LINCOLN COUNTY
P.O. Box 555
Brookhaven, MS 39601-0555
Phone: (601) 835-3479

MADISON COUNTY
P.O. Box 404
Canton, MS 39046-0404
Phone: (601) 859-1177

MARION COUNTY
250 Broad Street, Suite 2
Columbia, MS 39429
Phone: (601) 736-2691

MARSHALL COUNTY
P.O. Box 219
Holly Springs, MS 38635
Phone: (662) 252-4431

MONROE COUNTY
P.O. Box 578
Aberdeen, MS 39730-0578
Phone: (662) 369-8143

MONTGOMERY COUNTY
P.O. Box 71
Winona, MS 38967-0071
Phone: (662) 283-2333

NESHOBA COUNTY
401 Beacon Street
Philadelphia, MS 39350
Phone: (601) 656-6281

NEWTON COUNTY
P.O. Box 68
Decatur, MS 39327-0068
Phone: (601) 635-2367

NOXUBEE COUNTY
P.O. Box 147
Macon, MS 39341
Phone: (662) 726-4243

OKTIBBEHA COUNTY
101 East Main Street
Starkville, MS 39759
Phone: (662) 323-5834

PANOLA COUNTY
151 Public Square
Batesville, MS 38606
Phone: (662) 563-6201

PEARL RIVER COUNTY
P.O. Box 431
Poplarville, MS 39470-0431
Phone: (601) 795-2237

PERRY COUNTY
P.O. Box 198
New Augusta, MS 39462-0198
Phone: (601) 964-8398

PIKE COUNTY
218 East Bay Street, PO Box 431
Magnolia, MS 39652
Phone: (601) 783-5289

PONTOTOC COUNTY
P.O. Box 209
Pontotoc, MS 38863-0209
Phone: (662) 489-3900

QUITMAN COUNTY
230 Chestnut Street
Marks, MS 38646
Phone: (662) 326-2661

RANKIN COUNTY
305 Government Street
Brandon, MS 39042
Phone: (601) 825-1475

SCOTT COUNTY
P.O. Box 630
Forest, MS 39074-0630
Phone: (601) 469-1926

SHARKEY COUNTY
P.O. Box 218
Rolling Fork, MS 39159-0218
Phone: (662) 873-2755

SIMPSON COUNTY
P.O. Box 367
Mendenhall, MS 39114-0367
Phone: (601) 847-1418

SMITH COUNTY
P.O. Box 160
Raleigh, MS 39153
Phone: (601) 782-9811

STONE COUNTY
P.O. Drawer 7
Wiggins, MS 39577
Phone: (601) 928-5266

SUNFLOWER COUNTY
P.O. Box 988
Indianola, MS 38751-0988
Phone: (662) 887-4703

TALLAHATCHIE COUNTY
P.O. Box 350
Charelston, MS 38921
Phone: (662) 647-5551

TATE COUNTY
201 S. Ward Street
Senatobia, MS 38668-2616
Phone: (662) 562-5661

TIPPAH COUNTY
P.O. Box 99
Ripley, MS 38663-0099
Phone: (662) 837-7374

TISHOMINGO COUNTY
1008 Battleground Drive
Iuka, MS 38852
Phone: (662) 423-7032

TUNICA COUNTY
P.O. Box 639
Tunica, MS 38676-0639
Phone: (662) 363-1465

UNION COUNTY
P.O. Box 847
New Albany, MS 38652-0847
Phone: (662) 534-5284

WALTHALL COUNTY
P.O. Box 351
Tylertown, MS 39667-0351
Phone: (601) 876-3553

WARREN COUNTY
P.O. Box 351
Vicksburg, MS 39181-0351
Phone: (601) 636-4415

WASHINGTON COUNTY
P.O. Box 309
Greenville, MS 38702-0309
Phone: (662) 378-8355

WAYNE COUNTY
609 Azalea Drive
Waynesboro, MS 39367-1249
Phone: (662) 735-2873

WEBSTER COUNTY
P.O. Box 398
Walthall, MS 39771
Phone: (662) 258-4131

WILKINSON COUNTY
PO Box 1284
Woodville, MS 39669-0516
Phone: (601) 888-4381

WINSTON COUNTY
P.O. Drawer 69
Louisville, MS 39339
Phone: (662) 773-3631

YALOBUSHA COUNTY
P.O. Box 664
Water Valley, MS 38965-0664
Phone: (662) 473-2091

YAZOO COUNTY
P.O. Box 1106
Yazoo City, MS 39194-0068
Phone: (662) 746-2661

MISSOURI

**Missouri has a statutory penalty interest rate of 10%
Sale dates vary by county**

MISSOURI

ADAIR COUNTY
County Courthouse
106 North Washington Street
Kirksville, MO 63501
Phone: (660) 665-3350

ANDREW COUNTY
County Courthouse
PO Box 206
Savannah, MO 64485
Phone: (816) 324-3624

ATCHISON COUNTY
County Courthouse
PO Box 280
Rock Port, MO 64482
Phone: (660) 744-6214

BARRY COUNTY
County Courthouse
700 Main Street, Suite 2
Cassville, MO 65625
Phone: (417) 847-2561

BARTON COUNTY
County Courthouse
1004 Gulf
Lamar, MO 64759
Phone: (417) 682-3529

BATES COUNTY
County Courthouse
1 North Delaware Street
Butler, MO 64730
Phone: (660) 679-3371

BENTON COUNTY
County Courthouse
P.O. Box 1238
Warsaw, MO 65355-1238
Phone: (660) 438-7406
Fax: (660) 438-2062

BOLLINGER COUNTY
County Courthouse
P.O. Box 110
Marble Hill, MO 63764
Phone: (573) 238-2126
Fax: (573) 238-4511

BUTLER COUNTY
County Courthouse
105 Main Street
Poplar Bluff, MO 63901
Phone: (573) 686-8050

CALDWELL COUNTY
County Courthouse
P.O. Box 67
Kingston, MO 64650-0067
Phone: (816) 586-2571

CALLAWAY COUNTY
County Courthouse
10 East 5th Street
Fulton, MO 65251
Phone: (573) 642-0780

CAMDEN COUNTY
County Courthouse
1 Court Circle
Camdenton, MO 65020
Phone: (573) 346-4440

CARROLL COUNTY
County Courthouse
City Square
Carrollton, MO 64633
Phone: (660) 542-0615

CARTER COUNTY
County Courthouse
P.O. Box 517
Van Buren, MO 63965-0517
Phone: (573) 323-4527

CEDAR COUNTY
County Courthouse
P.O. Box 126
Stockton, MO 65785-0126

CHARITON COUNTY
County Courthouse
306 S Cherry
Keytesville, MO 65261
Phone: (660) 288-3273

CHRISTIAN COUNTY
County Courthouse
100 West Church
Ozark, MO 65721-0549
Phone: (417) 581-6360

CLARK COUNTY
County Courthouse
111 East Court Street
Kahoka, MO 63445
Phone: (660) 727-3283

CLAY COUNTY
County Courthouse
Courthouse Square
Liberty, MO 64068
Phone: (816) 792-7733

CLINTON COUNTY
County Courthouse
P.O. Box 245
Plattsburgh, MO 64477-0245
Phone: (816) 539-3713

COLE COUNTY
County Courthouse
301 East High
Jefferson City, MO 65101
Phone: (573) 634-9100

COOPER COUNTY
County Courthouse
200 Main Street
Boonville, MO 65233-1276
Phone: (660) 882-2114

CRAWFORD COUNTY
County Courthouse
P.O. Box AS
Steelville, MO 65565-0620
Phone: (573) 775-2376

DADE COUNTY
County Courthouse
Main Street
Greenfield, MO 65661
Phone: (417) 637-2724

DALLAS COUNTY
County Courthouse
P.O. Box 436
Buffalo, MO 65622-0436
Phone: (417) 345-2632

DAVIESS COUNTY
County Courthouse
102 North Main Street
Gallatin, MO 64640
Phone: (660) 663-2641

DEKALB COUNTY
County Courthouse
P.O. Box 248
Maysville, MO 64469-0248
Phone: (816) 449-5402

DENT COUNTY
County Courthouse
400 North Main Street
Salem, MO 65560-1436
Phone: (573) 729-4144

DOUGLAS COUNTY
County Courthouse
P.O. Box 398
Ava, MO 65608-0398
Phone: (417) 683-4714

DUNKLIN COUNTY
County Courthouse
P.O. Box 188
Kennett, MO 63857-0188
Phone: (573) 888-2796

GASCONADE COUNTY
County Courthouse
119 E. 1st Street
Hermann, MO 65041-1182
Phone: (573) 486-5427

GENTRY COUNTY
County Courthouse
200 Clay Street
Albany, MO 64402
Phone: (660) 726-3525

GRUNDY COUNTY
County Courthouse
700 Main Street
Trenton, MO 64683
Phone: (660) 359-6305

HARRISON COUNTY
County Courthouse
P.O. Box 525
Bethany, MO 64424
Phone: (660) 425-6424

HENRY COUNTY
County Courthouse
100 W. Franklin
Clinton, MO 64735
Phone: (660) 885-6953

HICKORY COUNTY
County Courthouse
P.O. Box 3
Hermitage, MO 65668-0003
Phone: (417) 745-6450

HOLT COUNTY
County Courthouse
P. O. Box 437
Oregon, MO 64473
Phone: (660) 446-3303

HOWARD COUNTY
County Courthouse
1 Courthouse Square
Fayette, MO 65248
Phone: (660) 248-3400

HOWELL COUNTY
County Courthouse
1 Courthouse Street
West Plains, MO 65775
Phone: (417) 256-2591

IRON COUNTY
County Courthouse
PO Box 42
Ironton, MO 63650
Phone: (573) 546-2912

JASPER COUNTY
County Courthouse
302 S. Main Street
Carthage, MO 64836
Phone: (417) 358-0421

JOHNSON COUNTY
County Courthouse
300 N. Holden Street
Warrensburg, MO 64093
Phone: (660) 747-2112

KNOX COUNTY
County Courthouse
107 N 4th Street
Edina, MO 63537
Phone: (660) 397-2184

LAFAYETTE COUNTY
County Courthouse
1001 Main Street
Lexington, MO 64067
Phone: (660) 259-4315

LAWRENCE COUNTY
County Courthouse
P.O. Box 309
Mount Vernon, MO 65712-0309
Phone: (417) 466-3666

LEWIS COUNTY
County Courthouse
P.O. Box 67
Monticello, MO 63457-0067
Phone: (573) 767-5205

LINCOLN COUNTY
County Courthouse
201 Main Street
Troy, MO 63379-1127
Phone: (636) 528-4415

LINN COUNTY
County Courthouse
P. O. Box 92
Lineus, MO 64653
Phone: (660) 895-5417

LIVINGSTON COUNTY
County Courthouse
700 Webster
Chillicothe, MO 64601
Phone: (660) 646-2293

MACON COUNTY
County Courthouse
PO Box 96
Macon, MO 63552
Phone: (660) 385-2913

MADISON COUNTY
County Courthouse
1 Court Square
Fredericktown, MO 63645
Phone: (573) 783-2176

MARIES COUNTY
County Courthouse
P. O. Box 205
Vienna, MO 65582
Phone: (573) 422-3388

MARION COUNTY
100 South Main Street
Palmyra, MO 63461
Phone: (573) 769-2549
Fax: (573) 769-4312

MCDONALD COUNTY
County Courthouse
P.O. Box 665
Pineville, MO 64856-0665
Phone: (417) 223-4717

MERCER COUNTY
County Courthouse
802 Main Street
Princeton, MO 64673
Phone: (660) 748-3425

MILLER COUNTY
County Courthouse
P.O. Box 12
Tuscumbia, MO 65082-0012
Phone: (573) 369-2317

MONITEAU COUNTY
County Courthouse
200 East Main
California, MO 65018
Phone: (573) 796-4661

MONROE COUNTY
County Courthouse
300 North Main Street
Paris, MO 65275-1399
Phone: (660) 327-5106

MONTGOMERY COUNTY
County Courthouse
211 East 3rd Street
Montgomery City, MO 63361-1956
Phone: (573) 564-3357

MORGAN COUNTY
County Courthouse
100 E Newton
Versailles, MO 65084
Phone: (573) 378-4644

NEW MADRID COUNTY
County Courthouse
P. O. Box 68
New Madrid, MO 63869
Phone: (573) 748-2524

NEWTON COUNTY
County Courthouse, 101 S Main
Neosho, MO 64850
Phone: (417) 451-8220

NODAWAY COUNTY
County Courthouse
P. O. Box 218
Maryville, MO 64468
Phone: (660) 582-2251

OREGON COUNTY
County Courthouse
P.O. Box 406
Alton, MO 65606-0324
Phone: (417) 778-4096

OSAGE COUNTY
County Courthouse
P.O. Box 826
Linn, MO 65051-0826
Phone: (573) 897-2139

OZARK COUNTY
County Courthouse
P.O. Box 416
Gainesville, MO 65655-0416
Phone: (417) 679-3516

PEMISCOT COUNTY
County Courthouse
610 Ward Avenue
Caruthersville, MO 63830
Phone: (573) 333-4203

PETTIS COUNTY
County Courthouse
415 South Ohio
Sedalia, MO 65301-4435
Phone: (660) 826-5395

PIKE COUNTY
County Courthouse
115 West Main Street
Bowling Green, MO 63334-1665
Phone: (573) 324-2412

POLK COUNTY
County Courthouse
102 East Broadway, Room 11
Bolivar, MO 65613
Phone: (417) 326-4031

PULASKI COUNTY
County Courthouse
301 Historic 66 East
Waynesville, MO 65583
Phone: (573) 774-4701

PUTNAM COUNTY
County Courthouse
Room 204, Main Street
Unionville, MO 63565
Phone: (660) 947-2674

RALLS COUNTY
County Courthouse
P. O. Box 400
New London, MO 63459
Phone: (573) 985-7111

RANDOLPH COUNTY
County Courthouse
110 South Main Street
Huntsville, MO 65259-1009
Phone: (660) 277-4717

RAY COUNTY
County Courthouse
100 West Main Street
Richmond, MO 64085
Phone: (816) 776-3184

REYNOLDS COUNTY
County Courthouse
P.O. Box 10
Centerville, MO 63633
Phone: (573) 648-2494

RIPLEY COUNTY
County Courthouse
Courthouse Circle
Doniphan, MO 63935
Phone: (573) 996-3215
Fax: (573) 996-501

SALINE COUNTY
County Courthouse
101 E Arrow Street
Marshall, MO 65340
Phone: (660) 886-3331

SCHUYLER COUNTY
County Courthouse
P.O. Box 187
Lancaster, MO 63548-0187
Phone: (660) 457-3842

SCOTLAND COUNTY
County Courthouse
117 South Market Street, Room 100
Memphis, MO 63555
Phone: (660) 465-7027

SCOTT COUNTY
County Courthouse
P. O. Box 188
Benton, MO 63736
Phone: (573) 545-3549

SHANNON COUNTY
County Courthouse
P.O. Box 187
Eminence, MO 65466-0187
Phone: (573) 226-3414

SHELBY COUNTY
County Courthouse
P.O. Box 186
Shelbyville, MO 63469-0186
Phone: (573) 633-2181

ST. CLAIR COUNTY
County Courthouse
P.O. Box 525
Osceola, MO 64776-0525
Phone: (417) 646-2315

ST. FRANCOIS COUNTY
County Courthouse
Courthouse Square
Farmington, MO 63640
Phone: (573) 756-3623

STODDARD COUNTY
County Courthouse
PO Box 110
Bloomfield, MO 63825
Phone: (573) 568-3339

STONE COUNTY
County Courthouse
P. O. Box 45
Galena, MO 65656
Phone: (417) 357-6127

SULLIVAN COUNTY
County Courthouse
109 North Main Street
Milan, MO 63556
Phone: (660) 265-3786

TEXAS COUNTY
County Courthouse
210 N. Grand Ave.
Houston, MO 65483
Phone: (417) 967-2112

VERNON COUNTY
County Courthouse
100 West Cherry
Nevada, MO 64772
Phone: (417) 448-2500

WARREN COUNTY
County Courthouse
104 W. Booneslick
Warrenton, MO 63383
Phone: (636) 456-3331

WAYNE COUNTY
County Courthouse
P. O. Box 48
Greenville, MO 63944
Phone: (573) 224-3011

WEBSTER COUNTY
County Courthouse
P.O. Box 529
Marshfield, MO 65706-0529

WORTH COUNTY
County Courthouse
P.O. Box 450
Grant City, MO 64456
Phone: (660) 564-2219

WRIGHT COUNTY
County Courthouse
P.O. Box 98
Hartville, MO 65667-0098
Phone: (417) 741-6661

MONTANA

Montana has a statutory penalty interest rate of 10%
Sale dates vary by county

MONTANA

BEAVERHEAD COUNTY
2 South Pacific Street
Dillon, MT 59725-2799
Phone: (406) 683-5245

BIG HORN COUNTY
121 3rd Street
Hardin, MT 59034-0908
Phone: (406) 665-3520

BLAINE COUNTY
400 Ohio
Chinook, MT 59523-0278
Phone: (406) 357-3250

BROADWATER COUNTY, MT
515 Broadway Street
Townsend, MT 59701-9256
Phone: (406) 266-3405

BUTTE-SILVER BOW COUNTY
155 West Granite Street
Butte, MT 59701-9256
Phone: (406) 723-8262

CARTER COUNTY
214 Park Street
Ekalaka, MT 59324-0315

CASCADE COUNTY
415 2nd Avenue
Great Falls, MT 59401-2537
Phone: (406) 454-6810

CHOUTEAU COUNTY
P.O. Box 459, 1308 Franklin
Fort Benton, MT 59442-0459
Phone: (406) 622-5151

CUSTER COUNTY
1010 Main Street
Miles City, MT 59301-3419
Phone: (406) 233-3343

DANIELS COUNTY
213 Main Street
Scobey, MT 59263-0247
Phone: (406) 487-5561

DAWSON COUNTY
207 W Bell Street
Glendive, MT 59330-1694
Phone: (406) 365-2022

FALLON COUNTY
P.O. Box 846
Baker, MT 59313-0846
Phone: (406) 778-7106

FERGUS COUNTY
712 West Main Street
Lewistown, MT 59457-2562
Phone: (406) 538-5119

FLATHEAD COUNTY
800 South Main Street
Kalispell, MT 59901-5400
Phone: (406) 758-5503

GALLATIN COUNTY
311 West Main Street
Bozeman, MT 59715-4576
Phone: (406) 582-3000

GARFIELD COUNTY
P.O. Box 7
Jordan, MT 59337-0007
Phone: (406) 557-2760

GLACIER COUNTY
512 Main Street
Cut Bank, MT 59427-3016
Phone: (406) 873-5063

GOLDEN VALLEY COUNTY
PO Box 10
Ryegate, MT 59074-0010
Phone: (406) 568-2231

GRANITE COUNTY
220 N Sansome
Philipsburg, MT 59858-0925
Phone: (406) 569-3771

HILL COUNTY
315 4th Street
Havre, MT 59501-3999
Phone: (406) 265-5481

JEFFERSON COUNTY
PO Box H, 201 Centennial
Boulder, MT 59632-0249
Phone: (406) 225-4000

LEWIS AND CLARK
316 North Park Avenue
Helena, MT 59624-1724
Phone: (406) 447-8000

LIBERTY COUNTY
111 1st Street East
Chester, MT 59522-0459
Phone: (406) 759-5365

LINCOLN COUNTY
512 California Avenue
Libby, MT 59923-1942
Phone: (406) 293-7781

MADISON COUNTY
101 W Wallace
Virginia City, MT 59755-0278
Phone: (406) 843-4270

MCCONE COUNTY
1004 Avenue C
Circle, MT 59215-0199
Phone: (406) 485-3500

MEAGHER COUNTY
15 W Main
White Sulphur Springs, MT 59645-0309
Phone: (406) 547-3612

MINERAL COUNTY
300 River Street
Superior, MT 59872-0550
Phone: (406) 822-4541

MISSOULA COUNTY
200 West Broadway
Missoula, MT 59802-4292
Phone: (406) 721-5700

MUSSELSHELL COUNTY
506 Main Street
Roundup, MT 59072-2498
Phone: (406) 323-1104

MUSSELSHELL COUNTY
506 Main Street
Roundup, MT 59072-2498
Phone: (406) 323-1104

PETROLEUM COUNTY
P.O. Box 226, 201 E Main
Winnett, MT 59087-0226
Phone: (406) 429-5551

PHILLIPS COUNTY
314 S 2nd Avenue West
Malta, MT 59538-0360
Phone: (406) 654-2429

PONDERA COUNTY
20 4th Avenue SW
Conrad, MT 59425-2340
Phone: (406) 278-4010

POWDER RIVER COUNTY
P.O. Box 270
Broadus, MT 59317-0270
Phone: (406) 436-2361

POWELL COUNTY
409 Missouri Avenue
Deer Lodge, MT 59722-1084
Phone: (406) 846-3680

PRAIRIE COUNTY
P.O. Box 125
Terry, MT 59349-0125
Phone: (406) 635-5575

RAVALLI COUNTY
205 Bedford Street, Box 5001
Hamilton, MT 58940-2853
Phone: (406) 375-6212

RICHLAND COUNTY
201 W. Main Street
Sidney, MT 59270-4087
Phone: (406) 482-1708

ROOSEVELT COUNTY
400 2nd Avenue South
Wolf Point, MT 59201-1600
Phone: (406) 653-6200

ROSEBUD COUNTY
P.O. Box 47
Forsyth, MT 59327-0047
Phone: (406) 356-7318

SANDERS COUNTY
P.O. Box 519
Thompson Falls, MT 59873-0519
Phone: (406) 827-4391

SHERIDAN COUNTY
100 W. Laurel Avenue
Plentywood, MT 59254-1619
Phone: (406) 765-2310

STILLWATER COUNTY
400 3rd Avenue North
Columbus, MT 59019-0970
Phone: (406) 322-8000

SWEET GRASS COUNTY
200 West First Avenue
Big Timber, MT 59011-0460
Phone: (406) 932-5152

TETON COUNTY
110 South Main Street
Choteau, MT 59422-0610
Phone: (406) 466-2151

TOOLE COUNTY
226 1st Street South
Shelby, MT 59474-1920
Phone: (406) 434-2232

TREASURE COUNTY
P.O. Box 392
Hysham, MT 59038-0392
Phone: (406) 342-5547

VALLEY COUNTY
501 Court Square, Box 1
Glasgow, MT 59230-2405
Phone: (406) 228-8221

WHEATLAND COUNTY
201 A Avenue NW
Harlowton, MT 59036-1903
Phone: (406) 632-4891
Fax: (406) 632-5654

WIBAUX COUNTY
200 S Wibaux
Wibaux, MT 59353-0199
Phone: (406) 796-2481

YELLOWSTONE COUNTY
217 N. 27th Street
Billings, MT 59107-5000
Phone: (406) 256-2701

NEBRASKA

Nebraska has a state statutory penalty interest rate of 14%.
This rate can vary by county.
Sale dates vary by county

NEBRASKA

ADAMS COUNTY
500 West Fifth, Room 109
Hastings, NE 68901-7509
Phone: (402) 461-7107

ANTELOPE COUNTY
501 Main Street
Neligh, NE 68756
Phone: (402) 887-4410

ARTHUR COUNTY
P.O. Box 126
Arthur, NE 69121-0126
Phone: (308) 764-2203

BANNER COUNTY
P.O. Box 67
Harrisburg, NE 69345-0067
Phone: (308) 436-5265

BLAINE COUNTY
P.O. Box 136
Brewster, NE 68821-0136
Phone: (308) 547-2222

BOONE COUNTY
222 South Fourth Street
Albion, NE 68620-1247
Phone: (402) 395-2055

BOX BUTTE COUNTY
P.O. Box 678
Alliance, NE 69301-0678
Phone: (308) 762-6565

BOYD COUNTY
County Courthouse
P.O. Box 26
Butte, NE 68722-0026
Phone: (402) 775-2391

BROWN COUNTY
148 W 4th
Ainsworth, NE 69210
Phone: (402) 387-2705

BUFFALO COUNTY
P.O. Box 1270
Kearney, NE 68848-1270
Phone: (308) 236-1224

BURT COUNTY
P.O. Box 87
Tekamah, NE 68061-0087
Phone: (402) 374-2955

BUTLER COUNTY
P.O. Box 289
David City, NE 68632-0289
Phone: (402) 367-3091

CASS COUNTY
346 Main Street
Plattsmouth, NE 68048-1964
Phone: (402) 296-9300

CEDAR COUNTY
P.O. Box 47
Hartington, NE 68739
Phone: (402) 254-7411

CHASE COUNTY
P.O. Box 1299
Imperial, NE 69033-1299
Phone: (308) 882-52
CHERRY COUNTY
P.O. Box 120
Valentine, NE 69201-0120
Phone: (402) 376-2420

CHEYENNE COUNTY
P.O. Box 217
Sidney, NE 69162-0217
Phone: (308) 254-2141

CLAY COUNTY
111 West Fairfield
Clay Center, NE 68933-1499
Phone: (402) 762-3463

Jim Yocom

COLFAX COUNTY
411 East 11th Street
Schuyler, NE 68661
Phone: (402) 352-3434

CUMING COUNTY
P.O. Box 290
West Point, NE 68788-0290
Phone: (402) 372-2144

CUMING COUNTY
P.O. Box 290
West Point, NE 68788-0290
Phone: (402) 372-2144

DAKOTA COUNTY
P.O. Box 39
Dakota City, NE 68731-0039
Phone: (402) 987-2130

DAWES COUNTY
451 Main Street
Chadron, NE 69337-2649
Phone: (308) 432-0100

DAWSON COUNTY
P.O. Box 370
Lexington, NE 68850-0370
Phone: (308) 324-2127

DEUEL COUNTY
P.O. Box 327
Chappell, NE 69129-0327
Phone: (308) 874-3308

DIXON COUNTY
P.O. Box 546
Ponca, NE 68770
Phone: (402) 755-2208

DODGE COUNTY
435 North Park
Fremont, NE 68025
Phone: (402) 727-2767

DOUGLAS COUNTY
1819 Farman Street
Omaha, NE 68102
Phone: (402) 444-7150

DUNDY COUNTY
P.O. Box 506
Benkelman, NE 69021-0506
Phone: (308) 423-2058

FILLMORE COUNTY
P.O. Box 307
Geneva, NE 68361-0307
Phone: (402) 759-4931

FRANKLIN COUNTY
County Courthouse
P.O. Box 146
Franklin, NE 68939-0146
Phone: (308) 425-6202

FRONTIER COUNTY
P.O. Box 40
Stockville, NE 69042-0040
Phone: (308) 367-8641

FURNAS COUNTY
P.O. Box 387
Beaver City, NE 68926-0387
Phone: (308) 268-4145

GAGE COUNTY
P.O. Box 429
Beatrice, NE 68310-0429
Phone: (402) 223-1300

GARDEN COUNTY
PO Box 486
Oshkosh, NE 69154-0486
Phone: (308) 772-3924

GARFIELD COUNTY
P.O. Box 218
Burwell, NE 68823-0218
Phone: (308) 346-4161

GOSPER COUNTY
P.O. Box 136
Elwood, NE 68937-0136
Phone: (308) 785-2611

GRANT COUNTY
P.O. Box 139
Hyannis, NE 69350-0139
Phone: (308) 458-2488

GREELEY COUNTY
P.O. Box 287
Greeley, NE 68842-0287
Phone: (308) 428-3625

HALL COUNTY
121 South Pine Street
Grand Island, NE 68801-6076
Phone: (308) 385-5080

HAMILTON COUNTY
1111 13th Street, Suite 1
Aurora, NE 68818
Phone: (402) 694-3443

HARLAN COUNTY
P.O. Box 698
Alma, NE 68920-0698
Phone: (308) 928-2173

HAYES COUNTY
P.O. Box 370
Hayes Center, NE 69032
Phone: (308) 286-3413

HITCHCOCK COUNTY
P.O. Box 248
Trenton, NE 69044-0248
Phone: (308) 334-5646

HOLT COUNTY
P.O. Box 329
O'Neill, NE 68763-0329
Phone: (402) 336-1762

HOOKER COUNTY
P.O. Box 184
Mullen, NE 69152-0184
Phone: (308) 546-2244

HOWARD COUNTY
P.O. Box 25
Saint Paul, NE 68873-0025
Phone: (308) 754-4343

JEFFERSON COUNTY
411 Fourth Street
Fairbury, NE 68352-2536
Phone: (402) 729-2323

JEFFERSON COUNTY
411 Fourth Street
Fairbury, NE 68352-2536
Phone: (402) 729-2323

KEARNEY COUNTY
P.O. Box 339
Minden, NE 68959
Phone: (308) 832-2723

KEITH COUNTY
P.O. Box 149
Ogallala, NE 69153-0149
Phone: (308) 284-4726

KEYA PAHA COUNTY
P.O. Box 349
Springview, NE 68778-0349
Phone: (402) 497-3791

KIMBALL COUNTY
114 East Third Street
Kimball, NE 69145-1401
Phone: (308) 235-2241

KNOX COUNTY
Main Street, Courthouse Square
Center, NE 68724
Phone: (402) 288-4282

LANCASTER COUNTY
555 South 10th Street, Room 110
Lincoln, NE 68508
Phone: (402) 441-7447

LINCOLN COUNTY
301 North Jeffers Street
North Platte, NE 69101
Phone: (308) 534-4350

LOGAN COUNTY
P.O. Box 8
Stapleton, NE 69163-0008
Phone: (308) 636-2311

LOUP COUNTY
P.O. Box 187
Taylor, NE 68879-0187
Phone: (308) 942-3135

MADISON COUNTY
110 Clara Davis Drive
Madison, NE 68748
Phone: (402) 454-3311

MCPHERSON COUNTY
P.O. Box 122
Tryon, NE 69167-0122
Phone: (308) 587-2363

MERRICK COUNTY
P.O. Box 27
Central City, NE 68826-0027
Phone: (308) 946-2881

MORRILL COUNTY
P.O. Box 610
Bridgeport, NE 69336-0610
Phone: (308) 262-0860

NANCE COUNTY
209 Esther Street
Fullerton, NE 68638
Phone: (308) 536-2331

NEMAHA COUNTY
1824 N Street
Auburn, NE 68305-2399
Phone: (402) 274-4213

NUCKOLLS COUNTY
PO Box 366
Nelson, NE 68961
Phone: (402) 225-4361

OTOE COUNTY
1021 Central Avenue
Nebraska City, NE 68410
Phone: (402) 873-9500

PAWNEE COUNTY
P.O. Box 431
Pawnee City, NE 68420-0431
Phone: (402) 852-2962

PERKINS COUNTY
P.O. Box 156
Grant, NE 69140-0156
Phone: (308) 352-4643

PHELPS COUNTY
P.O. Box 404
Holdrege, NE 68949-0404
Phone: (308) 995-4469

PIERCE COUNTY
111 W. Court Street
Pierce, NE 68767
Phone: (402) 329-4474

PLATTE COUNTY
2610 14th Street
Columbus, NE 68601
Phone: (402) 563-4904

POLK COUNTY
P. O. Box 276
Osceola, NE 68651
Phone: (402) 747-5431

RED WILLOW COUNTY
502 Norris Avenue
McCook, NE 69001
Phone: (308) 345-1552

RICHARDSON COUNTY
1700 Stone Street
Falls City, NE 68355
Phone: (402) 245-2911

ROCK COUNTY
400 State Street
Bassett, NE 68714
Phone: (402) 684-3933

SARPY COUNTY
1210 Golden Gate Drive
Papillion, NE 68046-2845
Phone: (402) 593-2100

SAUNDERS COUNTY
PO Box 61
Wahoo, NE 68066
Phone: (402) 443-8101

SCOTTS BLUFF COUNTY
1825 Tenth Street
Gering, NE 69341-2444
Phone: (308) 436-6600

SEWARD COUNTY
P.O. Box 190
Seward, NE 68434-0190
Phone: (402) 643-2883

SHERIDAN COUNTY
P.O. Box 39
Rushville, NE 69360-0039
Phone: (308) 327-2633

SHERMAN COUNTY
630 O Sytreet
Loup City, NE 68853
Phone: (308) 745-1513

SIOUX COUNTY
P. O. Box 158
Harrison, NE 69346
Phone: (308) 668-2443

STANTON COUNTY
P.O. Box 347
Stanton, NE 68779-0347
Phone: (402) 439-2222

THAYER COUNTY
P. O. Box 208
Hebron, NE 68370
Phone: (402) 768-6126

THOMAS COUNTY
503 Main Street
Thedford, NE 69166
Phone: (308) 645-2261

THURSTON COUNTY
P.O. Box G
Pender, NE 68047-0138
Phone: (402) 385-2343

VALLEY COUNTY
125 South 15th
Ord, NE 68862
Phone: (308) 728-3700

WASHINGTON COUNTY
1555 Colfax Street
Blair, NE 68008
Phone: (402) 426-6822

WAYNE COUNTY
P.O. Box 248
Wayne, NE 68787-0248
Phone: (402) 375-2288

WEBSTER COUNTY
621 North Cedar
Red Cloud, NE 68970
Phone: (402) 746-2716

WHEELER COUNTY
P. O. Box 127
Bartlett, NE 68622
Phone: (308) 654-3235

YORK COUNTY
510 Lincoln Avenue
York, NE 68467
Phone: (402) 362-7759

NEW HAMPSHIRE

New Hampshire has a penalty interest rate of 18%
Sale dates vary by county

NEW HAMPSHIRE

BELKNAP COUNTY
34 County Drive
Laconia, NH 03246-2900
Phone: (603) 524-3579

CARROLL COUNTY
PO Box 152
Ossipee, NH 03864-0152
Phone: (603) 539-2428

CHESHIRE COUNTY
33 West Street
Keene, NH 03431-3402
Phone: (603) 352-8215

COOS COUNTY
P.O. Box 10
West Stewartstown, NH 03597-0010
Phone: (603) 246-3321

GRAFTON COUNTY
RR 1, Box 67
North Haverhill, NH 03774-9758
Phone: (603) 787-6941

HILLSBOROUGH COUNTY
19 Temple Street
Nashua, NH 03060-3472
Phone: (603) 627-5600

MERRIMACK COUNTY
163 North Main Street
Concord, NH 03301
Phone: (603) 228-0331

ROCKINGHAM COUNTY
99-119 North Road
Brentwood, NH 03833
Phone: (603) 679-2256

STRAFFORD COUNTY
P.O. Box 799
Dover, NH 03821-0799
Phone: (603) 742-1458

SULLIVAN COUNTY
14 Main Street
Newport, NH 03773-1515
Phone: (603) 863-2560

NEW JERSEY

New Jersey has a penalty interest rate of 18%
Sale dates vary by county

NEW JERSEY

ATLANTIC COUNTY
5911 Main Street
Mays Landing, NJ 08330
Phone: (609) 645-5900

BERGEN COUNTY
21 Main Street
Hackensack, NJ 07601
Phone: (201) 336-6200

BURLINGTON COUNTY
49 Rancocas Road, PO Box 6000
Mount Holly, NJ 08060-6000
Phone: (609) 265-5020

CAMDEN COUNTY
520 Market Street, 16th Floor
Camden, NJ 08102
Phone: (856) 225-5354

CAPE MAY COUNTY
4 Moore Road
Cape May Court House, NJ 08210-1601
Phone: (609) 465-1065

CUMBERLAND COUNTY
790 East Commerce Street
Bridgeton, NJ 08302
Phone: (856) 453-2125

ESSEX COUNTY
465 Martin Luther King Blvd
Newark, NJ 07102-1705
Phone: (973) 621-4492

GLOUCESTER COUNTY
1 North Broad Street
Woodbury, NJ 08096-4611
Phone: (856) 853-3200

HUDSON COUNTY
583 Newark Avenue
Jersey City, NJ 07306-1803
Phone: (201) 795-6200

Hunterdon County
1 East Main Street, Victorian Plaza
Flemington, NJ 08822
Phone: (908) 788-1102

MERCER COUNTY
P.O. Box 8068
Trenton, NJ 08650-0068
Phone: (609) 989-6584

MIDDLESEX COUNTY
P.O. Box 871
New Brunswick, NJ 08903-0871
Phone: (732) 745-3000

MONMOUTH COUNTY
P.O. Box 1255
Freehold, NJ 07728-1255
Phone: (732) 431-7387

MORRIS COUNTY
P.O. Box 900
Morristown, NJ 07963-0900
Phone: (973) 285-6010

OCEAN COUNTY
101 Hooper Ave
Toms River, NJ 08754-2191
Phone: (732) 244-2121

SALEM COUNTY
92 Market Street
Salem, NJ 08079-1913
Phone: (856) 935-7510

SOMERSET COUNTY
P.O. Box 3000
Somerville, NJ 08876-1262
Phone: (908) 231-7030

SUSSEX COUNTY
County Administration Building
Plotts Road
Newton, NJ 07860
Phone: (973) 579-0210

UNION COUNTY
County Courthouse
2 Broad Street
Elizabeth, NJ 07207
Phone: (908) 527-4000

WARREN COUNTY
County County Courthouse
165 County Road, 519 South
Belvidere, NJ 07823-1949
Phone: (908) 475-6500

NEW YORK

New York has an interest rate of 18% plus a 5% penalty. However not all counties sell certificates.

Some counties have bundled certificates and sold them to large investors

NEW YORK

ALBANY COUNTY
112 State Street
Albany, NY 12207-2005
Phone: (518) 447-7300

ALLEGANY COUNTY
7 Court Street
Belmont, NY 14813
Phone: (716) 268-7612

BROOME COUNTY
P.O. Box 1766
Binghamton, NY 13902-1766
Phone: (607) 778-2109

CATTARAUGUS COUNTY
303 Court Street
Little Valley, NY 14755-1028
Phone: (716) 938-9111

CAYUGA COUNTY
160 Genesee Street
Auburn, NY 13021-3424
Phone: (315) 253-1308

CHAUTAUQUA COUNTY
Gerace Office Building
1 North Erie Street
Mayville, NY 14757

Phone: (716) 753-7111

CHEMUNG COUNTY
John H. Hazlett Building
203 Lake Street
Elmira, NY 14902-0588
Phone: (607) 737-2912

CHENANGO COUNTY
County Office Building
5 Court Street
Norwich, NY 13815
Phone: (607) 337-1430

CLINTON COUNTY
County Government Center
137 Margaret Street
Plattsburgh, NY 12901-2975
Phone: (518) 565-4600

COLUMBIA COUNTY
County Courthouse
401 State Street
Hudson, NY 12534-1915
Phone: (518) 828-1527

CORTLAND COUNTY
60 Central Avenue
Cortland, NY 13045
Phone: (607) 753-5052

DELAWARE COUNTY
111 Main Street
Delhi, NY 13753
Phone: (607) 746-6691

DUTCHESS COUNTY
22 Market Street
Poughkeepsie, NY 12601-3222
Phone: (914) 486-2020

ERIE COUNTY
25 Delaware Avenue
Buffalo, NY 14202-3903
Phone: (716) 858-7500

ESSEX COUNTY
P. O. Box 217
Elizabethtown, NY 12932
Phone: (518) 873-3700

FRANKLIN COUNTY
63 W. Main Street
Malone, NY 12953
Phone: (518) 483-6767

FULTON COUNTY
223 West Main Street
Johnstown, NY 12095
Phone: (518) 736-5555

GENESEE COUNTY
Main And Court Streets
Batavia, NY 14020
Phone: (716) 344-2550

GREENE COUNTY
Main Bridge Streets
Catskill, NY 12414-0467
Phone: (518) 943-2050

HAMILTON COUNTY
P. O. Box 205
Lake Pleasant, NY 12108
Phone: (518) 548-6651

HERKIMER COUNTY
109 Mary St, Ste 1310
Herkimer, NY 13350
Phone: (315) 867-1002

JEFFERSON COUNTY
175 Arsenal Street
Watertown, NY 13601-2522
Phone: (315) 785-3000

LEWIS COUNTY
7660 State Street
Lowville, NY 13367
Phone: (315) 376-5355

LIVINGSTON COUNTY
6 Court Street
Geneseo, NY 14454
Phone: (716) 243-7000

MADISON COUNTY
P.O. Box 668
Wampsville, NY 13163-0668
Phone: (315) 366-2011

MONROE COUNTY
39 West Main Street
Rochester, NY 14614
Phone: (716) 428-5301

MONTGOMERY COUNTY
P.O. Box 1500
Fonda, NY 12068-1500
Phone: (518) 853-3431

NASSAU COUNTY
County Courthouse
Mineola, NY 11501-4813
Phone: (516) 571-3000

NEW YORK CITY
52 Chamber Street
New York City, NY 10007
Phone: (212) 788-3000

NIAGARA COUNTY
County Courthouse
Lockport, NY 14094-2740
Phone: (716) 439-7000

ONEIDA COUNTY
800 Park Avenue
Utica, NY 13501-2939
Phone: (315) 798-5900

ONONDAGA COUNTY
407 Courthouse
Syracuse, NY 13202
Phone: (315) 435-2070

ONTARIO COUNTY
27 North Main Street
Canandaigua, NY 14424
Phone: (716) 396-4400

ORANGE COUNTY
255-275 Main Street
Goshen, NY 10924-1621
Phone: (845) 291-4000

ORLEANS COUNTY
3 South Main Street, Court House Square
Albion, NY 14411-1495
Phone: (716) 589-7053

OSWEGO COUNTY
46 E Bridge Street
Oswego, NY 13126
Phone: (315) 349-3235

OTSEGO COUNTY
197 Main Street
Cooperstown, NY 13326-1129
Phone: (607) 547-4200

PUTNAM COUNTY
40 Gleneida Avenue
Carmel, NY 10512-1798
Phone: (845) 225-3641

RENSSELAER COUNTY
1600 7th Avenue
Troy, NY 12180-3409

ROCKLAND COUNTY
11 New Hampstead Road
New City, NY 10956-3636
Phone: (845) 638-5100

SARATOGA COUNTY
County Municipal Center
40 McMasters Street
Ballston Spa, NY 12020-1986
Phone: (518) 885-5388

SCHENECTADY COUNTY
620 State Street
Schenectady, NY 12305-2114
Phone: (518) 388-4220

Schoharie County
P.O. Box 429
Schoharie, NY 12157-0429
Phone: (518) 295-8316

SCHUYLER COUNTY
105 Ninth Street
Watkins Glen, NY 14891
Phone: (607) 535-8100

SENECA COUNTY
1 DiPronio Drive
Waterloo, NY 13165-1680
Phone: (315) 539-5655

ST. LAWRENCE COUNTY
48 Court Street
Canton, NY 13617-1194
Phone: (315) 379-2276

SULLIVAN COUNTY
100 North Street
Monticello, NY 12701
Phone: (914) 794-3000

TIOGA COUNTY
56 Main Street
Owego, NY 13827
Phone: (607) 687-0100

TOMPKINS COUNTY
320 North Tioga Street
Ithaca, NY 14850
Phone: (607) 274-5434

ULSTER COUNTY
244 Fair Street Box 1800
Kingston, NY 12401-0800

WARREN COUNTY
1340 State Route 9
Lake George, NY 12845
Phone: (518) 761-6535

WASHINGTON COUNTY
Upper Broadway
Fort Edward, NY 12828
Phone: (518) 746-2210

WAYNE COUNTY
26 Church Street
Lyons, NY 14489
Phone: (315) 946-5400

WESTCHESTER COUNTY
148 Martine Avenue
White Plains, NY 10601-3311
Phone: (914) 285-2000

WYOMING COUNTY
143 North Main Street
Warsaw, NY 14569
Phone: (716) 786-8800

YATES COUNTY
110 Court Street
Penn Yan, NY 14527
Phone: (315) 536-5165

NORTH CAROLINA

The statutory penalty interest rate is 9%
The redemption period is six months

NORTH CAROLINA

ALAMANCE COUNTY
124 West Elm Street
Graham, NC 27253-2802
Phone: (336) 228-1312

ALEXANDER COUNTY
255 Liledoun Road
Taylorsville, NC 28681-2429
Phone: (828) 632-9332

ALLEGHANY COUNTY
P.O. Box 366
Sparta, NC 28675-0366
Phone: (336) 372-4179

ANSON COUNTY
Wadesboro, NC 28170
Phone: (704) 694-2796

ASHE COUNTY
150 Gov. Cir. Suite 2500
Jefferson, NC 28640-0633
Phone: (336) 246-1830

AVERY COUNTY
P.O. Box 640
Newland, NC 28657-0640
Phone: (828) 733-8201

BEAUFORT COUNTY
P.O. Box 1027
Washington, NC 27889-1027
Phone: (252) 946-0079

BERTIE COUNTY
108 Dundee Street
Windsor, NC 27983-0530
Phone: (252) 794-5300

BLADEN COUNTY
P.O. Box 1048
Elizabethtown, NC 28337-1048
Phone: (910) 862-6700

BRUNSWICK COUNTY
P.O. Box 249
Bolivia, NC 28422-0249
Phone: (910) 253-2000

BUNCOMBE COUNTY
60 Court Plaza
Ashville, NC 28801-3519
Phone: (828) 250-4001

BURKE COUNTY
200 Avery Avenue
Morganton, NC 28680-0219
Phone: (828) 439-4340

CABARRUS COUNTY
P.O. Box 707
Concord, NC 28026-0707
Phone: (704) 788-8100

CALDWELL COUNTY
P.O. Box 2200
Lenoir, NC 28645-2200
Phone: (828) 757-1111

CAMDEN COUNTY
P.O. Box 190
Camden, NC 27921-0190
Phone: (252) 338-1919

CARTERET COUNTY
Courthouse Square
Beaufort, NC 28516
Phone: (252) 728-8450

CASWELL COUNTY
P.O. Box 98
Yanceyville, NC 27379-0098
Phone: (336) 694-4193

CATAWBA COUNTY
P.O. Box 389
Newton, NC 28658-0389
Phone: (828) 465-8200

CHATHAM COUNTY
P.O. Box 87
Pittsboro, NC 27312-0087
Phone: (919) 542-8200

CHEROKEE COUNTY
701 Peachtree Street, Suite 112
Murphy, NC 28906-2900
Phone: (828) 837-5527

CHOWAN COUNTY
P.O. Box 1030
Edenton, NC 27932-1030
Phone: (252) 482-8431

CLAY COUNTY
P.O. Box 118
Hayesville, NC 28904-0118
Phone: (828) 389-0089

CLEVELAND COUNTY
P.O. Box 1210
Shelby, NC 28151-1210
Phone: (704) 484-4800

COLUMBUS COUNTY
111 Washington Street
Whiteville, NC 28472-3323
Phone: (910) 642-5700

CRAVEN COUNTY
302 Broad Street
New Bern, NC 28560
Phone: (252) 636-6600

CUMBERLAND COUNTY
P.O. Box 1829
Fayetteville, NC 28302-1829
Phone: (910) 678-7771

CURRITUCK COUNTY
P.O. Box 39
Currituck, NC 27929-0039
Phone: (252) 232-2075

DARE COUNTY
P.O. Box 1000
Manteo, NC 27954-1000
Phone: (252) 473-1101

DAVIDSON COUNTY
P.O. Box 1067
Lexington, NC 27293-1067
Phone: (336) 242-2000

DAVIE COUNTY
123 S. Main Street
Mocksville, NC 27028-2436
Phone: (336) 751-5513

DUPLIN COUNTY
P.O. Box 950
Kenansville, NC 28349-0910
Phone: (910) 296-2100

DURHAM COUNTY
200 East Main Street
Durham, NC 27701-3649
Phone: (919) 560-0000

EDGECOMBE COUNTY
P.O. Box 10
Tarboro, NC 27886-0010
Phone: (252) 641-7833

FORSYTH COUNTY
200 North Main Street
Winston-Salem, NC 27101
Phone: (336) 727-2797

Franklin County, NC
113 Market Street
Louisburg, NC 27549
Phone: (919) 496-5994

Gaston County
325 North Marietta Street
Gastonia, NC 28052
Phone: (704) 852-3100

GATES COUNTY
P.O. Box 148
Gatesville, NC 27938-0141
Phone: (252) 357-1240

GRAHAM COUNTY
P.O. Box 575
Robbinsville, NC 28771-0575
Phone: (828) 479-7961

GRANVILLE COUNTY
P.O. Box 906
Oxford, NC 27565-0906
Phone: (919) 693-5240

GREENE COUNTY
229 Kingold Blvd
Snow Hill, NC 28580
Phone: (252) 747-3446

GUILFORD COUNTY
P.O. Box 3427
Greensboro, NC 27402-3427
Phone: (336) 373-3383

HALIFAX COUNTY
P.O. Box 38
Halifax, NC 27839-0038
Phone: (252) 583-1131

HARNETT COUNTY
P.O. Box 759
Lillington, NC 27546-0759
Phone: (910) 893-7555

HAYWOOD COUNTY
215 North Main Street
Waynesville, NC 28786-3845
Phone: (828) 452-6625

HENDERSON COUNTY
100 N. King Street
Hendersonville, NC 28792-5097
Phone: (828) 697-4808

HERTFORD COUNTY
P.O. Box 116
Winton, NC 27986-0116
Phone: (252) 358-7805

HOKE COUNTY
Main Street
Raeford, NC 28376-0266
(910) 875-9222

HYDE COUNTY
P.O. Box 188
Swanquarter, NC 27885-0188
Phone: (252) 926-5711

IREDELL COUNTY
P.O. Box 788
Statesville, NC 28687-0788
Phone: (704) 878-3050

JACKSON COUNTY
401 Grindstaff Cove Road
Sylva, NC 28779-2922
Phone: (828) 586-4055

JOHNSTON COUNTY
P.O. Box 1049
Smithfield, NC 27577-1049
Phone: (919) 989-5100

JONES COUNTY
P.O. Box 266
Trenton, NC 28585-0266
Phone: (252) 448-7571

LEE COUNTY
PO Box 4209
Sanford, NC 27331-1968
Phone: (919) 718-4605

LENOIR COUNTY
P.O. Box 3289
Kinston, NC 28502-3289
Phone: (252) 523-7659

LINCOLN COUNTY
115 West Main Street
Lincolnton, NC 28092-2601
Phone: (704) 736-8473

MACON COUNTY
5 West Main Street
Franklin, NC 28734-3005
Phone: (828) 349-2025

MADISON COUNTY
P.O. Box 579
Marshall, NC 28753-0579
Phone: (828) 649-2521

MARTIN COUNTY
P.O. Box 668
Williamston, NC 27892-0668
Phone: (252) 792-1901

MCDOWELL COUNTY
60 East Court Street
Marion, NC 28752-4041
Phone: (828) 652-7121

MECKLENBURG COUNTY
600 East Fourth Street
Charlotte, NC 28231
Phone: (704) 336-2472

MITCHELL COUNTY
239 Crimson Laurel Way
Bakersville, NC 28705-0409
Phone: (828) 688-2139

MONTGOMERY COUNTY
P.O. Box 425
Troy, NC 27371-0425
Phone: (910) 576-4211

MOORE COUNTY
P.O. Box 905
Carthage, NC 28327-0905
Phone: (910) 947-6363

NASH COUNTY
County Courthouse
120 W. Washington St., Ste. 3072
Nashville, NC 27856
Phone: (252) 459-9800

NEW HANOVER COUNTY
320 Chestnut Street, Room 502
Wilmington, NC 28401-4027
Phone: (910) 341-7184

NORTHAMPTON COUNTY
PO Box 808
Jackson, NC 27845-0808
Phone: (252) 534-2501

ONSLOW COUNTY
625 Court Street
Jacksonville, NC 28540
Phone: (910) 455-4458

ORANGE COUNTY
P.O. Box 8181
Hillsborough, NC 27278-8181
Phone: (919) 732-8181

PAMLICO COUNTY
P.O. Box 776
Bayboro, NC 28515-0776
Phone: (252) 745-3133

PENDER COUNTY
P.O. Box 5
Burgaw, NC 28425-0005
Phone: (910) 259-1200

PERQUIMANS COUNTY
P.O. Box 45
Hertford, NC 27944-0045
Phone: (252) 426-8484

PERSON COUNTY
304 S. Morgan Street, Room 212
Roxboro, NC 27573-5245
Phone: (336) 597-1720

PITT COUNTY
100 West Third Street
Greenville, NC 27834
Phone: (252) 830-6300

POLK COUNTY
P.O. Box 308
Columbus, NC 28722-0308
Phone: (828) 894-3301

RANDOLPH COUNTY
145 Worth Street
Asheboro, NC 27203
Phone: (336) 318-6300

RICHMOND COUNTY
P.O. Box 504
Rockingham, NC 28380-0504
Phone: (910) 997-8200

ROBESON COUNTY
701 North Elm Street
Lumberton, NC 28358-4891
Phone: (910) 671-3022

ROCKINGHAM COUNTY
371 NC 65, Suite 206
Wentworth, NC 27375-0206
Phone: (336) 342-8100

ROWAN COUNTY
130 W Innes Street
Salisbury, NC 28144
Phone: (704) 636-0361

RUTHERFORD COUNTY
289 N. Main Street
Rutherfordton, NC 28139
Phone: (828) 287-6060

SAMPSON COUNTY
435 Rowan Road
Clinton, NC 28328-4700
Phone: (910) 592-6308

SCOTLAND COUNTY
P.O. Box 489
Laurinburg, NC 28353-0489
Phone: (910) 277-2406

STANLY COUNTY
201 S 2nd Street
Albemarle, NC 28001-5747
Phone: (704) 983-7200

STOKES COUNTY
P.O. Box 20
Danbury, NC 27016-0020
Phone: (336) 593-2811

SURRY COUNTY
118 Hamby Road
Dobson, NC 27017-8820
Phone: (336) 401-8201

SWAIN COUNTY
101 Mitchell Street
Bryson City, NC 28713-2001
Phone: (828) 488-9273

TRANSYLVANIA COUNTY
28 E. Main Street
Brevard, NC 28712-3738
Phone: (828) 884-3162

TYRRELL COUNTY
P.O. Box 449
Columbia, NC 27925-0449
Phone: (252) 796-1371

UNION COUNTY
500 N. Main Street, Room 921
Monroe, NC 28112
Phone: (704) 283-3810

VANCE COUNTY
122 Young Street, Suite B
Henderson, NC 27536-4292
Phone: (252) 738-2120

WAKE COUNTY
P.O. Box 550
Raleigh, NC 27602-0550
Phone: (919) 856-6160

WARREN COUNTY
P.O. Box 619
Warrenton, NC 27589-0619
Phone: (252) 257-3115

WASHINGTON COUNTY
P.O. Box 1007
Plymouth, NC 27962-1007
Phone: (252) 793-5823

WATAUGA COUNTY
842 West King Street
Boone, NC 28607-3525
Phone: (828) 265-8015

WAYNE COUNTY
P.O. Box 227
Goldsboro, NC 27533-0227
Phone: (919) 731-1435

WILKES COUNTY
Courthouse Square
Wilkesboro, NC 28697-2429
Phone: (336) 651-7300

WILSON COUNTY
P.O. Box 1728
Wilson, NC 27894-1728
Phone: (252) 399-2803

YADKIN COUNTY
P.O. Box 146
Yadkinville, NC 27055-0146
Phone: (336) 679-4200

YANCEY COUNTY
Room 11
Burnsville, NC 28714
Phone: (828) 682-3819

Jim Yocom

NORTH DAKOTA

North Dakota has a penalty interest rate of 12%
Sale dates are second Tuesday of December, but can vary
Redemption period is three years

NORTH DAKOTA

ADAMS COUNTY
602 Adams Avenue
Hettinger, ND 58639
Phone: (701) 567-2468

BARNES COUNTY
230 4th Street, NW
Valley City, ND 58072-2947
Phone: (701) 845-8500

BENSON COUNTY
311 B Avenue South
Minnewauken, ND 58351-0206
Phone: (701) 473-5340

BILLINGS COUNTY
495 4th Street
Medora, ND 58645-0168
Phone: (701) 623-4377

BOTTINEAU COUNTY
314 West 5th Street
Bottineau, ND 58318-1204
Phone: (701) 228-2225

BOWMAN COUNTY
104 1st Street NW
Bowman, ND 58623
Phone: (701) 523-5421

BURKE COUNTY
4001 Main Street
Bowbells, ND 58721-0310
Phone: (701) 377-2875

CASS COUNTY
211 Ninth Street South, Box 2806
Fargo, ND 58108
Phone: (701) 241-5609

CAVALIER COUNTY
901 3rd Street
Langdon, ND 58249-2457
Phone: (701) 256-2229

DICKEY COUNTY
309 North 2nd
Ellendale, ND 58436-0215
Phone: (701) 349-3249

DIVIDE COUNTY
300 Second Avenue
Crosby, ND 58730-0049
Phone: (701) 965-6351

DUNN COUNTY
P.O. Box 105
Manning, ND 58642-0105
Phone: (701) 573-4448

EDDY COUNTY
524 Central Avenue
New Rockford, ND 58356-1698
Phone: (701) 947-2434

EMMONS COUNTY
P.O. Box 129
Linton, ND 58552-0129
Phone: (701) 254-4807

FOSTER COUNTY
1000 North Central Avenue
Carrington, ND 58421-0104
Phone: (701) 652-2441

GOLDEN VALLEY COUNTY
150 1st Avenue
Beach, ND 58621
Phone: (701) 872-4331

GRAND FORKS COUNTY
124 South 4th Street
Grand Forks, ND 58201-4782
Phone: (701) 780-8200

GRANT COUNTY
P.O. Box 227
Carson, ND 58529-0227

GRIGGS COUNTY
808 Rollin Avenue, SW
Cooperstown, ND 58425
Phone: (701) 797-3117

HETTINGER COUNTY
339 Pacific Avenue
Mott, ND 58646
Phone: (701) 824-2515

KIDDER COUNTY
120 East Broadway
Steele, ND 58482
Phone: (701) 475-2632

LAMOURE COUNTY
202 4th Avenue, NE
La Moure, ND 58458
Phone: (701) 883-5301

LOGAN COUNTY
301 Broadway
Napoleon, ND 58561
Phone: (701) 754-2425

MCHENRY COUNTY
P.O. Box 147
Towner, ND 58788-0147
Phone: (701) 537-5724

MCINTOSH COUNTY
112 NE 1st NE
Ashley, ND 58413
Phone: (701) 288-3347

MCKENZIE COUNTY
PO Box 543
Watford City, ND 58854-0543
Phone: (701) 444-3616

MCLEAN COUNTY
712 5th Avenue
Washburn, ND 58577
Phone: (701) 462-8541

MCLEAN COUNTY
712 5th Avenue
Washburn, ND 58577
Phone: (701) 462-8541

MERCER COUNTY
P.O. Box 39
Stanton, ND 58571-0039
Phone: (701) 745-3292

MORTON COUNTY
210 2nd Avenue, NW
Mandan, ND 58554-3124
Phone: (701) 667-3300

MOUNTRAIL COUNTY
P.O. Box 69
Stanley, ND 58784-0069
Phone: (701) 628-2145

NELSON COUNTY
210 West B Avenue, PO Box 585
Lakota, ND 58344-0585
Phone: (701) 247-2463

OLIVER COUNTY
115 Main Street
Center, ND 58530
Phone: (701) 794-8777

PEMBINA COUNTY
301 Dakota Street, W
Cavalier, ND 58220
Phone: (701) 265-4231

PIERCE COUNTY
240 SE 2nd Street
Rugby, ND 58368-1830
Phone: (701) 776-5225

RAMSEY COUNTY
524 4th Avenue
Devils Lake, ND 58301
Phone: (701) 662-7007

RANSOM COUNTY
P.O. Box 668
Lisbon, ND 58054-0668
Phone: (701) 683-5823

RENVILLE COUNTY
205 Main Street East
Mohall, ND 58761
Phone: (701) 756-6301

RICHLAND COUNTY
418 2nd Avenue, N.
Wahpeton, ND 58075-4400
Phone: (701) 642-7700
ROLETTE COUNTY
P.O. Box 939
Rolla, ND 58367-0939
Phone: (701) 477-5665

SARGENT COUNTY
355 Main Street
Forman, ND 58032-0177
Phone: (701) 724-6241

SHERIDAN COUNTY
P.O. Box 636
McClusky, ND 58463-0636
Phone: (701) 363-2205

SIOUX COUNTY
302 2nd Avenue
Fort Yates, ND 58538
Phone: (701) 854-3481

SLOPE COUNTY
206 S Main
Amidon, ND 58620
Phone: (701) 879-6276

STARK COUNTY
51 3rd Street East
Dickinson, ND 58601
Phone: (701) 264-7630

STEELE COUNTY
P.O. Box 275
Finley, ND 58230-0275
Phone: (701) 524-2110

STUTSMAN COUNTY
511 2nd Avenue
Jamestown, ND 58401
Phone: (701) 252-9035

TOWNER COUNTY
2nd Street And 4th Avenue
Cando, ND 58324
Phone: (701) 968-4340

TRAILL COUNTY
P.O. Box 429
Hillsboro, ND 58045-0429
Phone: (701) 436-4458

WALSH COUNTY
600 Cooper Avenue
Grafton, ND 58237
Phone: (701) 352-2851

WARD COUNTY
P.O. Box 5005
Minot, ND 58702-5005
Phone: (701) 857-6420

WELLS COUNTY
P.O. Box 37
Fessenden, ND 58438-0037
Phone: (701) 547-3521

WILLIAMS COUNTY
P.O. Box 2047
Williston, ND 58802-2047
Phone: (701) 572-1700

OKLAHOMA

Oklahoma has a statutory penalty interest rate of 8%
Sale dates vary by county

OKLAHOMA

ALFALFA COUNTY
300 South Grand Street
Cherokee, OK 73728
Phone: (580) 596-3158

ATOKA COUNTY
200 East Court Street
Atoka, OK 74525
Phone: (580) 889-5157

BEAVER COUNTY
P.O. Box 338
Beaver, OK 73932-0338
Phone: (480) 625-4742

BECKHAM COUNTY
P.O. Box 428
Sayre, OK 73662
Phone: (580) 928-2457

BLAINE COUNTY
P.O. Box 138
Watonga, OK 73772-0138
Phone: (580) 623-5890

BRYAN COUNTY
PO Box 1789
Durant, OK 74702
Phone: (580) 924-2201

CADDO COUNTY
P.O. Box 68
Anadarko, OK 73005
Phone: (405) 247-6609

CANADIAN COUNTY
PO Box 458
El Reno, OK 73036
Phone: (405) 422-2422

CARTER COUNTY
P.O. Box 1236
Ardmore, OK 73005
Phone: (580) 223-5290

CHEROKEE COUNTY
213 W. Delaware, Room 200
Tahlequah, OK 74464
Phone: (918) 456-2261

CHOCTAW COUNTY
300 East Duke
Hugo, OK 74743-4009
Phone: (580) 326-3778

CIMARRON COUNTY
P.O. Box 145
Boise City, OK 73933-0145
Phone: (580) 544-2251

CLEVELAND COUNTY
201 South Jones Street
Norman, OK 73069-6046
Phone: (405) 366-0200

COAL COUNTY
4 North Main Street, Suite 3
Coalgate, OK 74538
Phone: (580) 927-3122

COMANCHE COUNTY
315 SW 5th Street
Lawton, OK 73501-9026
Phone: (580) 353-3717

COTTON COUNTY
301 North Broadway
Walters, OK 73572-1271
Phone: (580) 875-3026

CRAIG COUNTY
P.O. Box 397
Vinita, OK 74301-0397
Phone: (918) 256-7559

CREEK COUNTY
317 E Lee, Suite 100
Sapulpa, OK 74066
Phone: (918) 224-3529

CUSTER COUNTY
P.O. Box 300
Arapahoe, OK 73620-0300
Phone: (580) 323-4420

DELAWARE COUNTY
P.O. Box 309
Jay, OK 74346
Phone: (918) 253-4520

DEWEY COUNTY
P.O. Box 368
Taloga, OK 73667-0368
Phone: (580) 328-5668

ELLIS COUNTY
P.O. Box 197
Arnett, OK 73832
Phone: (580) 885-7301

GARFIELD COUNTY
PO Box 1664
Enid, OK 73702
Phone: (580) 237-0225

GARVIN COUNTY
P.O. Box 167
Pauls Valley, OK 73075
Phone: (405) 238-3303

GRADY COUNTY
326 West Choctaw Street
Chickasha, OK 73018
Phone: (405) 224-5211

GRANT COUNTY
112 Guthrie, Room 104
Medford, OK 73759
Phone: (580) 395-2862

GREER COUNTY
P.O. Box 207
Mangum, OK 73554-0207
Phone: (580) 782-2307

HARMON COUNTY
114 West Hollis Street
Hollis, OK 73550
Phone: (580) 688-3658

HARPER COUNTY
P.O. Box 369
Buffalo, OK 73834-0369
Phone: (580) 735-2870

HASKELL COUNTY
202 East Main Street
Stigler, OK 74462-2439
Phone: (918) 967-8792

HUGHES COUNTY
200 N. Broadway Street, Suite 7
Holdenville, OK 74848-3400
Phone: (405) 379-6739

JACKSON COUNTY
101 North Main Street, 101
Altus, OK 73521-3142
Phone: (580) 482-2370

JEFFERSON COUNTY
220 North Main, Room 101
Waurika, OK 73573
Phone: (580) 228-2029

JOHNSTON COUNTY
403 W Main
Tishomingo, OK 73460
Phone: (580) 371-3058

KAY COUNTY
P.O. Box 450,
201 S. Main
Newkirk, OK 74647-0450
Phone: (580) 362-2130

KINGFISHER COUNTY
101 South Main, Room 3
Kingfisher, OK 73750
Phone: (405) 375-3818

KIOWA COUNTY
316 South Main, Box 653
Hobart, OK 73651
Phone: (580) 726-3377

LATIMER COUNTY
109 N Central
Wilburton, OK 74578
Phone: (918) 465-4002

LE FLORE COUNTY
P.O. Box 607
Poteau, OK 74953-0607
Phone: (918) 647-3701

LINCOLN COUNTY
811 Manvel Avenue
Chandler, OK 74834
Phone: (405) 258-0080

LOGAN COUNTY
301 East Harrison
Guthrie, OK 73044
Phone: (405) 282-1900

LOVE COUNTY
405 West Main Street
Marietta, OK 73448
Phone: (580) 276-3059

MAJOR COUNTY
P.O. Box 379
Fairview, OK 73737-0379
Phone: (580) 227-4520

MARSHALL COUNTY
One Courthouse Square, Room 101
Madill, OK 73446
Phone: (580) 795-3165

MAYES COUNTY
P.O. Box 95
Pryor, OK 74362-0095
Phone: (918) 825-0639

MCCLAIN COUNTY
P.O. Box 629
Purcell, OK 73080-0629
Phone: (405) 527-3117

MCCURTAIN COUNTY
P.O. Box 1078
Idabel, OK 74745-1078
Phone: (580) 286-7428

MCINTOSH COUNTY
P.O. Box 110
Eufaula, OK 74432-0110
Phone: (918) 689-2452

MURRAY COUNTY
P.O. Box 240
Sulphur, OK 73086-0240
Phone: (580) 622-3777

MUSKOGEE COUNTY
P.O. Box 2307
Muskogee, OK 74402-2307
Phone: (918) 682-2169

NOBLE COUNTY
300 Courthouse Drive 1
Perry, OK 73077-0409
Phone: (580) 336-2771

NOWATA COUNTY
229 N. Maple Street
Nowata, OK 74048-2654
Phone: (918) 273-0175

OKFUSKEE COUNTY
P.O. Box 108
Okemah, OK 74859
Phone: (918) 623-0105

OKLAHOMA COUNTY
320 Robert S. Kerr Avenue, Room 105
Oklahoma City, OK 73102
Phone: (405) 270-0082

OKMULGEE COUNTY
PO Box 904
Okmulgee, OK 74447
Phone: (918) 756-2365

PAWNEE COUNTY
500 Harrison, Room 202
Pawnee, OK 74058
Phone: (918) 762-2732

PAYNE COUNTY
PO Box 7
Stillwater, OK 74076
Phone: (405) 747-8338

PITTSBURGH COUNTY
PO Box 3304
McAlester, OK 74502
Phone: (918) 423-6865

PONTOTOC COUNTY
P.O. Box 1425
Ada, OK 74820-1425
Phone: (405) 332-1425

POTTAWATOMIE COUNTY
325 N. Broadway Street
Shawnee, OK 74801-6938
Phone: (405) 273-4305

PUSHMATAHA COUNTY
302 SW B Street
Antlers, OK 74523
Phone: (580) 298-3626

ROGER MILLS COUNTY
P.O. Box 708
Cheyenne, OK 73628-0708
Phone: (580) 497-3330

ROGERS COUNTY
PO Box 1210
Claremore, OK 74018
Phone: (918) 341-3965

SEMINOLE COUNTY
110 S Wewoka, Suite 103
Wewoka, OK 74884
Phone: (405) 257-2450

SEQUOYAH COUNTY
120 East Chickasaw
Sallisaw, OK 74955
Phone: (918) 775-5539

STEPHENS COUNTY
101 South 11th Street, Room 100
Duncan, OK 73533
Phone: (580) 255-4193

TEXAS COUNTY
P.O. Box 197
Guymon, OK 73942-0197
Phone: (580) 338-7644

TILLMAN COUNTY
P.O. Box 992
Frederick, OK 73542-0992
Phone: (580) 335-3421

TULSA COUNTY
500 South Denver
Tulsa, OK 74103
Phone: (918) 596-5780

WAGONER COUNTY
PO Box 156
Wagoner, OK 74477
Phone: (918) 485-2142

WASHINGTON COUNTY
420 S. Johnstone Avenue, Room 108
Bartlesville, OK 74003-6602
Phone: (918) 337-2850

WASHITA COUNTY
P.O. Box 380
Cordell, OK 73632-0380
Phone: (580) 832-3548

WOODS COUNTY
407 Government
Alva, OK 73717
Phone: (580) 327-2126

SOUTH DAKOTA

South Dakota has a statutory penalty interest rate of 12%

Sale dates can vary by county but are usually the third Monday Of December

SOUTH DAKOTA

AURORA COUNTY
P.O. Box 513
Plankinton, SD 57368
Phone: (605) 942-7586

BEADLE COUNTY
P.O. Box 845
Huron, SD 57350-0845
Phone: (605) 352-8436

BENNETT COUNTY
P.O. Box 460
Martin, SD 57551-0460
Phone: (605) 685-6969

BON HOMME COUNTY
300 West 18th Avenue
Tyndall, SD 57066
Phone: (605) 589-4212

BROOKINGS COUNTY
314 6th Avenue
Brookings, SD 57006
Phone: (605) 692-6284

BROWN COUNTY
25 Market Street
Aberdeen, SD 57401-4293
Phone: (605) 626-7109

BRULE COUNTY
300 South Courtland
Chamberlain, SD 57325
Phone: (605) 734-6521

BUFFALO COUNTY
P. O. Box 146
Gann Valley, SD 57341-0146
Phone: (605) 293-3217

BUTTE COUNTY
839 Fifth Ave
Belle Fourche, SD 57717-1719
Phone: (605) 892-4485

CAMPBELL COUNTY
P.O. Box 37
Mound City, SD 57646-0037
Phone: (605) 955-3366

CHARLES MIX COUNTY
P.O. Box 490
Lake Andes, SD 57356-0490
Phone: (605) 487-7131

CLARK COUNTY
P.O. Box 294
Clark, SD 57225-0294
Phone: (605) 532-5921

CLAY COUNTY
211 W. Main Street, Suite 200
Vermillion, SD 57069-2039
Phone: (605) 677-7120

CODINGTON COUNTY
14 First Avenue SE
Watertown, SD 57201-3611
Phone: (605) 882-6297

CORSON COUNTY
P.O. Box 255
Mc Intosh, SD 57641-0255
Phone: (605) 273-4229

CUSTER COUNTY
420 Mount Rushmore Road
Custer, SD 57730-1934
Phone: (605) 673-4815

DAVISON COUNTY
200 East 4th Avenue
Mitchell, SD 57301-2631
Phone: (605) 995-8608

DAY COUNTY
710 West First Street
Webster, SD 57274-1391
Phone: (605) 345-3102

DEUEL COUNTY
P.O. Box 616
Clear Lake, SD 57226-0616
Phone: (605) 874-2312

DEWEY COUNTY
Main Street
Timber Lake, SD 57656
Phone: (605) 865-3672

DOUGLAS COUNTY
County Courthouse
P.O. Box 159
Armour, SD 57313-0159
Phone: (605) 724-2423

EDMUNDS COUNTY
P.O. Box 97
Ipswich, SD 57451-0097
Phone: (605) 426-6762

FALL RIVER COUNTY
906 North River Street
Hot Springs, SD 57747-1387
Phone: (605) 745-5130

FAULK COUNTY
P.O. Box 309
Faulkton, SD 57438-0309
Phone: (605) 598-6224

GRANT COUNTY
210 East 5th Avenue
Milbank, SD 57252
Phone: (605) 432-6711

GREGORY COUNTY
P.O. Box 413
Burke, SD 57523-0413
Phone: (605) 775-2664

HAAKON COUNTY
PO Box 698
Philip, SD 57567-0698
Phone: (605) 859-2800

HAMLIN COUNTY
P.O. Box 237
Hayti, SD 57241-0237
Phone: (605) 783-3201

HAND COUNTY
415 West First Avenue
Miller, SD 57362-1346
Phone: (605) 853-2182

HANSON COUNTY
P.O. Box 67
Alexandria, SD 57311-0067
Phone: (605) 239-4714

HARDING COUNTY
P.O. Box 26
Buffalo, SD 57720-0026
Phone: (605) 375-3313

HUGHES COUNTY
104 E. Capitol Avenue
Pierre, SD 57501-2563
Phone: (605) 773-7477

HUTCHINSON COUNTY
140 Euclid Room 128
Olivet, SD 57052-0128
Phone: (605) 387-2835

HYDE COUNTY
P.O. Box 379
Highmore, SD 57345-0379
Phone: (605) 852-2519

JACKSON COUNTY
P.O. Box 280
Kadoka, SD 57543-0280
Phone: (605) 837-2422

JERAULD COUNTY
PO Box 422
Wessington Springs, SD 57382-0422
Phone: (605) 539-9301

KINGSBURY COUNTY
202 2nd Street, SE
De Smet, SD 57231
Phone: (605) 854-3832

LAKE COUNTY
200 East Center
Madison, SD 57042-2956
Phone: (605) 256-7600

LAWRENCE COUNTY
90 Sherman Street
Deadwood, SD 57732-1370
Phone: (605) 578-1941

LINCOLN COUNTY
100 East Fifth Street
Canton, SD 57013-1798
Phone: (605) 987-2581

LYMAN COUNTY
P.O. Box 38
Kennebec, SD 57544-0038
Phone: (605) 869-2247

MARSHALL COUNTY
P.O. Box 130
Britton, SD 57430-0130
Phone: (605) 448-2401

MCCOOK COUNTY
P.O. Box 190
Salem, SD 57058-0190
Phone: (605) 425-2791

MCPHERSON COUNTY
P.O. Box L
Leola, SD 57456-0448
Phone: (605) 439-3314

MEADE COUNTY
1425 Sherman Street
Sturgis, SD 57785-1452
Phone: (605) 347-2360

MELLETTE COUNTY
P.O. Box C
White River, SD 57579-0703
Phone: (605) 259-3291

MINER COUNTY
401 N. Main Street
Howard, SD 57349-0086
Phone: (605) 772-4671

MINNEHAHA COUNTY
415 N. Dakota Avenue
Sioux Falls, SD 57104-2465
Phone: (605) 367-4206

MOODY COUNTY
P.O. Box 152
Flandreau, SD 57028-0152
Phone: (605) 997-3161

PENNINGTON COUNTY
315 St. Joseph Street
Rapid City, SD 57701-2879
Phone: (605) 394-2171

PERKINS COUNTY
P.O. Box 126
Bison, SD 57620-0126
Phone: (605) 244-5624

POTTER COUNTY
201 South Exene
Gettysburg, SD 57442
Phone: (605) 765-9408

ROBERTS COUNTY
411 2nd Avenue East
Sisseton, SD 57262
Phone: (605) 698-3395

SANBORN COUNTY
604 W 6th Street, PO Box 7
Woonsocket, SD 57385-0007
Phone: (605) 796-4513

SHANNON COUNTY
906 North River Street
Hot Springs, SD 57747-1387
Phone: (605) 745-3996

SPINK COUNTY
210 East 7th Avenue
Redfield, SD 57469-1299
Phone: (605) 472-1825

STANLEY COUNTY
P.O. Box 595
Fort Pierre, SD 57532-0595
Phone: (605) 223-2673

SULLY COUNTY
P.O. Box 265
Onida, SD 57564-0265
Phone: (605) 258-2541

TODD COUNTY
200 East Third Street
Winner, SD 57580
Phone: (605) 856-3727

TURNER COUNTY
P.O. Box 370
Parker, SD 57053-0370
Phone: (605) 297-3153

UNION COUNTY
P.O. Box 519
Elk Point, SD 57025-0519
Phone: (605) 356-2041

WALWORTH COUNTY
P.O. Box 199
Selby, SD 57472-0199
Phone: (605) 649-7878

YANKTON COUNTY
PO Box 137
Yankton, SD 57078

ZIEBACH COUNTY
P.O. Box 68
Dupree, SD 57623-0068
Phone: (605) 365-5157

WEST VIRGINIA

West Virginia has a statutory penalty interest rate of 12%

Sale dates vary by counties

WEST VIRGINIA

BARBOUR COUNTY
8 North Main Street
Philippi, WV 26416
Phone: (304) 457-2232

BERKELEY COUNTY
126 West King Street
Martinsburg, WV 25401
Phone: (304) 264-1923

BOONE COUNTY
206 Court Street
Madison, WV 25130
Phone: (304) 369-3925

BRAXTON COUNTY
PO Box 486
Sutton, WV 26601
Phone: (304) 765-2835

BROOKE COUNTY
632 Main Street
Wellsburg, WV 26070-1743
Phone: (304) 737-3661

CABELL COUNTY
750 5th Avenue
Huntington, WV 25701-2072
Phone: (304) 526-8625

CALHOUN COUNTY
P.O. Box 230
Grantsville, WV 26147-0230
Phone: (304) 354-6725

CLAY COUNTY
P.O. Box 190
Clay, WV 25043-0190
Phone: (304) 587-4259

DODDRIDGE COUNTY
118 East Court Street
West Union, WV 26456-1297
Phone: (304) 873-2631

FAYETTE COUNTY
P.O. Box 307
Fayetteville, WV 25840-0307
Phone: (304) 574-4014
Fax: (304) 574-4255

GILMER COUNTY
10 Howard Street
Glenville, WV 26351
Phone: (304) 462-7641

GRANT COUNTY
5 Highland Avenue
Petersburg, WV 26847-1705
Phone: (304) 257-4550

GREENBRIER COUNTY
P.O. Box 506
Lewisburg, WV 24901-0506
Phone: (304) 647-6602

HAMPSHIRE COUNTY
P.O. Box 806
Romney, WV 26757-0806
Phone: (304) 822-5112

HANCOCK COUNTY
102 North Court Street
New Cumberland, WV 26047-9400
Phone: (304) 564-3311

HARDY COUNTY
204 Washington Street, Room 111
Moorefield, WV 26836
Phone: (304) 538-2929

HARRISON COUNTY
301 West Main Street
Clarksburg, WV 26301-2909
Phone: (304) 624-8611

JACKSON COUNTY
P.O. Box 800
Ripley, WV 25271
Phone: (304) 372-2011

JEFFERSON COUNTY
P.O. Box 250
Charles Town, WV 25414-0250
Phone: (304) 728-3284

KANAWHA COUNTY
PO Box 3627
Charleston, WV 25336
Phone: (304) 357-0101

LEWIS COUNTY
P.O. Box 87
Weston, WV 26452-0087
Phone: (304) 269-8200

LINCOLN COUNTY
P.O. Box 497
Hamlin, WV 25523
Phone: (304) 824-7990

LOGAN COUNTY
300 Stratton Street
Logan, WV 25601
Phone: (304) 792-8600

MARSHALL COUNTY
P.O. Box 459
Moundsville, WV 26041-0459
Phone: (304) 845-1220

MASON COUNTY
200 6th Street
Point Pleasant, WV 25550
Phone: (304) 675-1997

MCDOWELL COUNTY
90 Wyoming Street, Suite 111
Welch, WV 24801-2487
Phone: (304) 436-8544

MINGO COUNTY
P.O. Box 1197
Williamson, WV 25661-1197
Phone: (304) 235-0381

MONROE COUNTY
P.O. Box 350
Union, WV 24983-0350
Phone: (304) 772-3096

MORGAN COUNTY
PO Box 28
Berkeley Springs, WV 25411
Phone: (304) 258-8540

NICHOLAS COUNTY
700 Main Street
Summersville, WV 26651
Phone: (304) 872-7830

OHIO COUNTY
1500 Chapline Street
Wheeling, WV 26003-3553
Phone: (304) 234-3628

PENDLETON COUNTY
P.O. Box 187
Franklin, WV 26807
Phone: (304) 358-2505

PLEASANTS COUNTY
301 Court Lane, Suite 101
Saint Marys, WV 26170
Phone: (304) 684-7542

POCAHONTAS COUNTY
900C 10th Street
Marlinton, WV 24954-1310
Phone: (304) 799-4549

PRESTON COUNTY
101 West Main Street
Kingwood, WV 26537-1198
Phone: (304) 329-1805

PUTNAM COUNTY
3389 Winfield Road
Winfield, WV 25213
Phone: (304) 586-0202

RALEIGH COUNTY
215 Main Street
Beckley, WV 25801
Phone: (304) 255-9146

RANDOLPH COUNTY
P.O. Box 368
Elkins, WV 26241-0368
Phone: (304) 636-0543

RITCHIE COUNTY
115 East Main Street, Room 201
Harrisville, WV 26362
Phone: (304) 643-2164

ROANE COUNTY
P.O. Box 69
Spencer, WV 25276-0069
Phone: (304) 927-2860

SUMMERS COUNTY
P.O. Box 97
Hinton, WV 25951-0066
Phone: (304) 466-7100

TAYLOR COUNTY
214 West Main Street
Grafton, WV 26354
Phone: (304) 265-1401

TUCKER COUNTY
215 1st Street
Parsons, WV 26287
Phone: (304) 478-2866

TYLER COUNTY
P.O. Box 66
Middlebourne, WV 26149-0066
Phone: (304) 758-2102

UPSHUR COUNTY
38 West Main Street
Buckhannon, WV 26201
Phone: (304) 472-1068

WAYNE COUNTY
P.O. Box 248
Wayne, WV 25570-0248
Phone: (304) 272-6369

WEBSTER COUNTY
2 Court Square, Room G-1
Webster Springs, WV 26288
Phone: (304) 847-2508

WETZEL COUNTY
P.O. Box 156
New Martinsville, WV 26155-0156
Phone: (304) 455-8224

WIRT COUNTY
P.O. Box 53
Elizabeth, WV 26143-0053
Phone: (304) 275-4271

WOOD COUNTY
1 Court Square
Parkersburg, WV 26101
Phone: (304) 424-1850

WYOMING COUNTY
P.O. Box 309
Pineville, WV 24874-0309
Phone: (304) 732-8000

WYOMING

Wyoming has a statutory penalty interest rate of 18%

Sale dates vary by county

WYOMING

ALBANY COUNTY
Grand Avenue
Laramie, WY 82070
Phone: (307) 721-2541

BIG HORN COUNTY
420 C Street
Basin, WY 82410
Phone: (307) 568-2357

CAMPBELL COUNTY
500 South Gillette Avenue
Gillette, WY 82716-4239
Phone: (307) 682-7283

CARBON COUNTY
P.O. Box 6
Rawlins, WY 82301-0006
Phone: (307) 328-2668

CONVERSE COUNTY
107 North 5th Street, Suite 114
Douglas, WY 82633
Phone: (307) 358-2244

CROOK COUNTY
P.O. Box 37
Sundance, WY 82729-0037
Phone: (307) 283-1323

FREMONT COUNTY
450 North Second - Room 220
Lander, WY 82520-2337
Phone: (307) 332-2405

GOSHEN COUNTY
P.O. Box 160
Torrington, WY 82240-0160
Phone: (307) 532-4051
Fax: (307) 532-7375

HOT SPRINGS COUNTY
415 Arapahoe
Thermopolis, WY 82443-2731
Phone: (307) 864-3515

JOHNSON COUNTY
76 North Main Street
Buffalo, WY 82834-1847
Phone: (307) 684-7555

LARAMIE COUNTY
310 West 19th Street, Suite 300
Cheyenne, WY 82001
Phone: (307) 633-4260

LINCOLN COUNTY
925 Sage Avenue
Kemmerer, WY 83101
Phone: (307) 877-9056

NATRONA COUNTY
P.O. Box 863
Casper, WY 82602-0863
Phone: (307) 235-9202

NIOBRARA COUNTY
424 S. Elm, Box 420
Lusk, WY 82225-0420
Phone: (307) 334-2211

PARK COUNTY
1002 Sheridan Avenue
Cody, WY 82414-3532
Phone: (307) 527-8500

PLATTE COUNTY
P.O. Box 728
Wheatland, WY 82201-0728
Phone: (307) 322-3555

SHERIDAN COUNTY
244 S. Main
Sheridan, WY 82801
Phone: (307) 674-6722

SUBLETTE COUNTY
P.O. Box 250
Pinedale, WY 82941-0250
Phone: (307) 367-4372

SWEETWATER COUNTY
P.O. Box 730
Green River, WY 82935-0730
Phone: (307) 875-9360

TETON COUNTY
P.O. Box 3594
Jackson, WY 83001
Phone: (307) 733-4430

UINTA COUNTY
225 9th Street
Evanston, WY 82930
Phone: (307) 783-0301

WASHAKIE COUNTY
P.O. Box 260
Worland, WY 82401-0260
Phone: (307) 347-6491

WESTON COUNTY
1 West Main Street
Newcastle, WY 82701-2106
Phone: (307) 746-2684

About the Author

Jim Yocom has been involved in the real estate investment business for over twenty-five years. He has been the Director of Sales for a large multi-state land development company. He has owned his own real estate company. He is the author of SET YOURSELF FREE an investment training program. He has toured the United States, holding seminars to teach people how to invest in real estate with no money down and how to benefit from financial planning based on real estate investments. He has appeared on radio and television as a nationally known real estate investment authority.

Printed in the United States
1452500001B/280